BEST RESUMES FOR ACCOUNTANTS AND FINANCIAL PROFESSIONALS

Kim Marino

John Wiley & Sons, Inc.

New York ▪ Chichester ▪ Brisbane ▪ Toronto ▪ Singapore

Library of Congress Cataloging in Publication Data:

Marino, Kim, 1951–
    Best resumes for accountants and financial professionals / by
Kim Marino.
        p.   cm.
    ISBN 0-471-59542-X. — ISBN 0-471-59543-8 (pbk.)
    1. Accounting—Vocational guidance.   2. Résumés (Employment)
I. Title.
HF5627.M33   1993
657'.023'73—dc20   93-18206

Preface

As the founder of Just Resumes® and author of four resume books, including *Just Resumes®* (John Wiley, November 1991), and *Resumes for the Health Care Professional* (John Wiley, January 1993), I am readily acquainted with the resume needs of accountants and financial professionals. My files contain resume samples from a wide range of accounting professionals, administrators, and chief executive officers, allowing me to stay in touch with this dynamic field and bring this knowledge to bear in this book.

Best Resumes for Accountants and Financial Professionals includes well over 80 resume samples for public, corporate, and government accountants as well as for those changing careers from certified public accountant (CPA) to administrator, chief financial officer (CFO), and chief executive officer (CEO). The book covers both traditional and newly created positions. This step-by-step guide, which will teach you the fine art of creating a professionally designed resume, contains many examples from my vast bank of accounting and financial professional resumes. I have also provided valuable tips and facts that are specific to the accounting profession.

In addition, you will find cover letters, thank-you letter samples, and how-to information to complete the resume packet. Later chapters offer job tips and descriptions of specific key jobs, job trends, and job search techniques. I have included tough questions asked in the interview and examples of answers the interviewer wants to hear.

Whether you're an accounting professional moving up the ladder of success, changing careers, or returning to the work force; or a college student or recent graduate entering the accounting industry, this book is one of the best investments you'll ever make.

KIM MARINO

Fort Collins, Colorado
January 1994

Acknowledgments

I'd like to express my gratitude to the following accountant and financial professionals who have been instrumental in helping me with my research in the accounting industry: Jim Varlamos, Vice President, Key Banks of Colorado; Mike West, Director of Human Resources, Arthur Andersen & Co.; Rhonda Trimble, CPA and Director, Source Finance®; Donna Chapel, CPA, Sample & Bailey, Certified Public Accountants, PC; Andrea Smith, Society of Certified Public Accountants; Jean Wightman, Employment Manager, Colorado State University, Office of Personnel; Joseph R. DeLoy, Denver Service Center Director, U.S. Office of Personnel Management; Dana Klausmeyer, Controller, Larimer County Finance Department; Carl Conti, Personnel Specialist, State of Colorado, Department of Personnel; Rhonda Rodriquez, CPA; Dan Lauber, Planning Communications; Charles Davidshofer, PhD, Director of Counseling and Career Services, Colorado State University. I'd also like to thank Martin Perlman for so graciously giving me moral support.

K.M.

Contents

Contents

1

The Professional Resume

Whether you are on your way to becoming a Chief Executive Officer or starting out new in the field as a recent graduate, accounting is an exciting profession. Every business—large or small, public, private, finance, or government—needs a good accountant. Some professionals concentrate on one phase of accounting; for example, many public accountants work primarily in auditing (examining a client's financial records and reporting to investors and authorities that the records have been prepared and reported correctly). Others concentrate on tax matters, such as preparing individual income tax returns and advising companies of the tax advantages and disadvantages of certain business decisions. And some accountants concentrate on consulting and offer advice on matters such as the design of companies' accounting and data-processing systems and controls to safeguard assets. Whatever your interest, this profession allows you to specialize in any area of accounting and work in any industry in the world—manufacturing, communications, finance, education, health care, entertainment. Practically every firm needs one or more financial managers-partner, treasurer, controller, credit manager, cash manager, and others.

For those of you interested in changing careers, Chapter 3 of *Best Resumes for Accountants and Financial Professionals* describes many professions that call for your valuable accountant skills, such as hospital administrator, director of human resources, or securities analyst.

A resume is something you should have in your back pocket, ready to give out at a moment's notice. Why? Because you'll never know when that special job opportunity may open up for you. Your resume is a custom designed, self-marketing tool tailored to your career objectives. A professional resume functions in four ways:

1. It focuses the interviewer's attention on *your* strongest points.
2. It give you full credit for all your achievements, whether you were paid or not.
3. It guides the interviewer toward positive things to talk about in *you*, and, in the direction you want to go.
4. Most importantly, because it lets *you* see yourself in a more focused and positive manner, it puts you in control of your own future. (It's also the first link between you and the potential employer. No wonder there's so much pressure on job seekers to create an effective resume!)

Many resumes in this book are from actual accounting professionals who have been clients of Just Resumes®. Others were created for this book with accurate job descriptions and educational requirements. They are examples of the kind of resume you, with the help of this book, are going to create. Many of these clients came to me with skills and education similar to yours. Working with them, I was able to produce a personalized resume that genuinely reflected their needs, accomplishments, and goals.

Before you leap into the resume-writing process, please take a few minutes to obtain an overview of my approach for creating a professional resume. Read the first two chapters: "The Professional Resume" and "The Straightforward Approach to Resume Writing," and then go through any of the next group of chapters that might apply to you. In Chapter 3, you'll find information on changing careers or making a lateral move. Chapter 4 shows you how to move up in the field you are in. And Chapter 5 offers suggestions for the recent graduate. If you haven't done so already, next turn to the resume samples in Chapter 11 to see how all the theory behind resume writing can be turned into fact.

Reading the introductory chapters and surveying actual resumes will prime you for writing your own resume. You will also want to begin analyzing your own background and pinpointing your targeted career. What you have done in previous positions or gained through education and what you want to do in your career will also influence the format you are going to use. You might go with the traditional chronological format that highlights your job history. You may wish to emphasize your skills by using the highly flexible functional format. Or you may opt to use a combination of the chronological and functional formats, which is a way of highlighting a specific job or skill while also indicating other previous jobs.

My step-by-step instructions and examples will prompt and guide you in creating your resume. Whichever format you decide to use, your aim should be to capture your strongest qualities, focused on your new job objective. Your professional style resume will show the interviewer and/or potential employer you are qualified for that desired position. When you have completed your first draft, review this book's first two chapters, compare what you've written with the resumes I've included, and revise your own resume as necessary.

If your previous experiences with resume writing have been more frustrating than fun, you are not alone. Perhaps under a looming job interview deadline, you tried to put something together only to have the resume turn out flat and uninviting or scattered and unfocused.

Tip: Lack of focus on your future job objective is the number one reason most resumes fail. All too often, people begin a resume with the wrong focus and either cannot complete it or else end up with an unsatisfactory product.

I help my clients at Just Resumes® concentrate on *where* they are going, rather than where they have been or where they are now. In doing so, they create resumes that still make use of their experience, but in a way that amplifies and directs their skills and experiences toward a specific goal. If you focus on your job objective, not only will your resume point you in the right direction, it also will show the potential employer how the past and present qualify you for that job.

TIPS FOR PUBLIC, PRIVATE, AND FINANCE ACCOUNTANTS AND AUDITORS

Tip 1   The Big Six accounting firms employ three types of accountants at one of five levels. The three types are auditor, tax, and consultant; the five levels are Staff, Senior, Manager, Partner and Senior Partner, or Partner in Charge.

Tip 2   Most public accounting firms have a *focus* that can be very different from one region of the country to another, even within the same organization. For example, the oil and gas industry may be very strong in Houston, Texas, whereas Denver's focus may be the ski industry. This is largely because many large cities (such as New York, Houston, and Chicago) have more Fortune 500 corporations than smaller cities (such as Denver), which—as a result—tend to focus mostly on smaller businesses.

Tip 3   Those of you who enjoy traveling on the job may choose to work for one of the Big Six accounting firms, such as Arthur Andersen. If you're employed in the Denver office and specialize in the oil and gas industry, the company might send you to another office—for example, Houston or the Middle East—to work on a project in your area of expertise.

Tip 4   Typically, the Fortune 500 corporations have four types of accountants: internal auditing, tax accounting, general accounting, and cost accounting. The five levels are Staff, Senior, Manager, Assistant Controller, and Controller, or Chief Accounting Executive (CAE).

Tip 5   Finance corporations typically have three types of accountants: credit analyst, financial planner/analyst, and cash management. The five levels are Staff, Senior, Manager, Treasurer, and Chief Financial Officer (CFO), or Vice President-Finance.

TIPS FOR ALL ACCOUNTING PROFESSIONAL JOB SEEKERS

This may be hard to believe, but many job applications live or die in the first 30 seconds of the screening process. It's in that 30-second glance that the receptionist or applications examiner decides either to forward your resume to the next step or reject it. Several strategies, however, can increase your chances of having your resume reach the interviewer.

Tip 1   Limit your resume to one or two pages. Almost all the resume samples in this book are one page in length. Because they are concise and to the point, the resumes clearly convey the writers' abilities and strengths. If you have so much experience that one page will not suffice, use two pages to get the job done, but in any case, don't try the faulty approach of using a smaller and smaller typeface to cram all the information onto one page. You don't want to make the employer's job any tougher than it is by handing in a hard-to-read resume.

Tip 2   Your educational background always goes at the end of the resume unless you are a recent graduate and your degree is stronger than your experience, or you are applying for a position at an educational institution.

Tip 3   Be objective. I advise clients to have an objective on their resumes, even a general objective. Faced with dozens of applications each day, the person doing the initial screening does not have the time to determine what position you're applying for at the organization or firm. You'll also look more focused, and in turn more desirable for the position, than those whose resumes lack the objective. Their loss is your gain.

Tip 4   If you are an experienced accountant but are unsure which specific area of accounting you'd like to work in or if you're a recent graduate and haven't decided which area you'd like to enter, it's best to say under objective, "A position in the accounting profession." This focuses you in accounting, but if something special opens up, you may also be considered for that position. Some firms will start accountants in specialty areas right out of college, but many do not. There is more about this is Chapter 5.

Consider this incident from Just Resumes. A woman contacted me whose resume had been prepared by another professional resume writer. She was receiving responses but for the wrong jobs. When I examined her materials, I saw that the objective was in her cover letter but not in her resume. In reading the resume (without an objective), I could see how she appeared to be qualified for several jobs, even though she was only interested in one. We worked together, adding a job objective and rewriting the resume so that its components pointed directly to that objective. With a revised resume, now focused on her objective, she received a positive response from the very company she'd written to previously, but this time for the position she desired.

RESUME CHARACTERISTICS

As mentioned earlier, there are three basic resume formats: chronological, functional, and combination. The chronological format, which is written in reverse chronological order, emphasizes your jobs. The functional style highlights your skills, with a lesser emphasis on the job titles. A combination approach uses the strengths of both the chronological and the functional styles.

Most of you are already familiar with the chronological format, the more traditional style. The functional, chronological, and combination resumes all should offer the same information; the difference is in how the information is presented, in what is emphasized.

PERSONAL DATA

With today's equal opportunity requirements, personal data are not required, indeed do not belong, on a resume. Personnel agencies have admitted to me that they've seem examples of prejudice from the persons screening resumes. Sometimes the screener may not even be aware of it.

SUMMARY OF RESUME STYLES

- ► The chronological format highlights the progress you've made in your jobs.
- ► The functional format highlights your skills.
- ► The combination format combines the chronological and functional formats to highlight selected jobs.

THE RESUME APPEARANCE: READY, GET SET, TYPE

The typeface you select is almost as important as the format you use for your resume. With today's ever-expanding computer typefaces, the choices can be overwhelming. To simplify the matter, opt for a typeface that looks professional and is easy to read; it should enhance but not dominate your overall resume presentation (see the resume samples in Chapter 11). Avoid the temptation to use a fancy script style; more effective are such tested stalwarts as Helvetica, Century Schoolbook, or Univers, which are all available through laser printing and desktop publishing on both the Macintosh and IBM computer systems. The type size should be no smaller than 11 point.

Don't scrimp when selecting resume paper—color and texture are the key factors. For the accounting professional, a brilliant white conveys a sense of competence, although ivory and light grey work well too. Whether you're a certified public accountant or chief financial officer, your personal preference plays a part in this, too.

You can choose among many different textured papers. Parchment has a light textured background woven into the paper; classic laid, which also works great with resumes, has a heavier smooth woodlike finished look; classic linen has a lighter clothlike texture; and cotton, the most expensive, feels and looks just like cotton fabric. As with the typeface you choose, the resume paper should complement your resume, *not* dominate it. Resume paper and matching envelopes are available at your local copy shop.

RESUME DO'S AND DON'TS

- ► DO choose a job that you "love."
- ► DO spend time listing all your good qualities. This is where you get credit where credit's due.
- ► DO include a clear and concise job objective; focus on your objective to show the employer how the past and present qualify you for that job.
- ► DO include experience directly related to the objective.
- ► DO start each sentence with a vigorous action word.
- ► DO list all related experience, paid or unpaid if you're a recent graduate or are reentering the work force. Include experience from community service, internships, and/or volunteer work.
- ► DO research the position and organization before the interview.
- ► DO keep your resume down to one or two pages.
- ► DO follow up the interview with a personalized thank-you letter.

- ► DON'T leave out the job objective.
- ► DON'T include material or history unrelated to the job objective.
- ► DON'T use long, repetitive explanations.
- ► DON'T include personal history.
- ► DON'T presume that the "personnel screener" understands skills included in the job title—tailor your job description.
- ► DON'T take for granted skills that you perform well as a matter of course.
- ► DON'T replace a job description with a job title—it's not self-explanatory. An auditor in one firm may not have the same responsibilities as an auditor at another organization.
- ► DON'T forget to include your grade point average (GPA) under education, if you're a student or recent graduate and it's 3.5 or higher.
- ► DON'T list references unless you have previously received permission or a positive response.
- ► DON'T send a "form" thank-you letter. Personalize each one.
- ► DON'T *be afraid to show off your skills.*

2

The Straightforward
Approach to
Resume Writing

A professionally designed resume conveys a significant amount of information concisely and vigorously. Straightforward, single-line phrases and sentences are easy to read and direct the employer's attention toward your capabilities and desired experiences. If you prefer paragraph form, that can be quite effective, although one-liners are more quickly noticed and understood. In either case, begin each key phrase with an action word, such as *developed* or *implemented*, to describe what you do (see list, "More than 100 Action Words," at the end of this chapter).

Action words energize your resume, but avoid using the same one twice within one job description or, if using the functional format, twice in the Professional Experience section. In a functional resume, you will create subsections, the titles of which will depend on the skills you are highlighting for a specific job objective (see resume samples, Chapter 11).

REMEMBER: ALWAYS THINK POSITIVE AND FOCUS THE RESUME ON YOUR JOB OBJECTIVE.

THE BASIC RESUME ELEMENTS

Whether you decide to use the chronological, functional, or combination format will depend on the way you want to present your information. Your own background and your objective will determine which resume style will work best. No matter what the format, however, each resume should offer the same basic information.

The resume you will create—functional, combination, or chronological—will incorporate these basic sections:

- ▶ Name, address, and phone number.
- ▶ Career objective.
- ▶ Professional profile (optional).
- ▶ Education and certification.
- ▶ Affiliations.
- ▶ Description of work experience.
- ▶ Employment history with job title, organization name, location, and dates of employment.

Remember:

- ▶ All key phrases start with a vigorous action verb.
- ▶ All job descriptions and experiences focus on the career objective.
- ▶ Education is placed after "Professional Experience," unless you are applying for an accounting position with an educational institution or organization, or you are a recent college graduate with limited work experience.

PREPARING THE CHRONOLOGICAL RESUME

The traditional chronological resume combines your experience and the employment history under one section. You list each position including the dates of employment, job title, organization name, city, and state, and follow it with a point-by-point description of job experience. Jobs are listed in reverse order beginning with the most recent position.

The chronological resume highlights the progress in your jobs. Because of this, it works best for professionals who are making an upward career move in the accounting profession. For example, an assistant controller for a large manufacturing firm is being considered for a position as controller. The previous positions held by the person show a steady progression toward that goal. A chronological resume, with appropriate job descriptions, would perfectly represent career growth and development leading to this latest position.

Use the chronological resume format when all three of the following points apply to you:

1. Your entire employment history shows progress with skills related to your objective. (Let's say you began your career as a staff auditor for a public accounting firm, moving up first to senior auditor and then to audit manager. Now you're aiming for Partner, which follows directly from your previous experience.)

2. Each position involves a generally different job description. (Each position—from Staff Auditor to Audit Manager—incorporates more responsibility and different job descriptions. The Staff Auditor performs the detail work of a financial audit under the supervision of a Senior. The Senior Auditor works under the general direction of an Audit Manager. Responsibilities include the direction of audit field work, assignment of detail work to Staff, and review of their working papers. Senior Auditors also prepare financial statements, develop corporate tax returns and suggest improvements to internal controls. The Audit Manager supervises Seniors and Staff and is responsible for audit program approval, personnel scheduling, audit working papers review, financial statement disclosure footnote approval, day-to-day client relationships, determination of billings for engagements, and training and evaluation of Staff and Seniors.)

3. Your work history is stable.

If your job history reflects these points and you are aiming for a position that seems to follow your previous career path, then create a chronological resume:

1. List your name, address, and phone number. (College students: Include your campus and permanent address, if you have one.)

2. State your objective: Make it brief and to the point. *Example:* A Budget Analyst position.

3. Provide a profile—a brief description or summary of your skills, personality traits, and achievements related to the job objective. What are personality traits? These are your particular characteristics that demonstrate your talents and abilities on the job. *Example:* Assume you want to be a Senior Financial Planner/Analyst. The interviewer will look for

someone who can pay close attention to detail and maintain good communication skills under strict deadline schedules.

4. Describe your education: degree (BA, MA), major, school, graduation date. When you become certified, make sure to include this information here.

5. State your professional experience or related experience. What date did you start your present job? (year starting/ ending). What organization (name, city, and state) do you presently work for? Describe what you did at each job. Include any special achievements you've accomplished, related to your objective. Always focus on your strongest points, directly related to your career objective. Be consistent and provide the preceding information under experience for each position pertinent to your objective. Look at resume samples for more details.

Example:

Auditor   1989–present

Contract Audit Agency, Santa Barbara, CA

- Performs audits of small and intermediate contractors throughout Santa Barbara as an active member of the mobile team.
- Evaluates proposals to determine reasonableness, accuracy, and compliance with government regulations.
- Reviews contractors' labor charging and allocation system to determine the adequacy of contractors' labor policies, procedures, and internal controls.
- Recommends improvements to comply with government regulations.
- Analyzes contractors' accounting systems and internal controls to determine adequacy of accumulating and segregating costs for government contracts.

For more variations on the Professional Experience section, consult the chronological resume samples in Chapter 11.

Once you have created the segment for your present job, repeat the procedure for each of your previous job experiences.

PREPARING THE FUNCTIONAL RESUME

Even at a glance, a functional resume looks different from a chronological resume. Because the functional format highlights your skills, it denotes a great deal more space to describing your experience. Such sections might include Management and Administration, Cost Accounting, Auditing, and Taxation to name a few. Conversely, the actual employment history will be listed at the end of the resume and will concisely give the basic information as to job title, locations, and dates.

In the functional resume:

▶ All the work experience appears in subsections created to highlight skills geared toward the job objective.

▶ The entire employment history is listed at the end of the resume with job title, organization name, city, state, and dates of employment, each job in reverse chronological order, but without a detailed explanation of the experience.

If you are changing careers, are a first-time job seeker, or are reentering the job market, the functional resume works best. Does the following information sound similar to your own background?

1. Your entire work history goes beyond the skills and experience related to your objective.
2. You have skills related to your job objective but not necessarily in your employment history.
3. You've had several positions with the same job description.

A functional resume is designed to be selective. If your entire work history includes additional skills not related to your career objective, you'll only highlight those skills pertinent to your objective, and if you've had several positions with the same job description, you don't need to repeat yourself. You'll only say what you did one time, which saves both space on the resume for other valuable information and time for the resume examiner. Don't worry that you might be minimizing your achievements, because you will, of course, list the jobs that cover similar experience under Previous Employment History (see functional resume samples, Chapter 11). As you become familiar with the functional resume, you'll see how it can convey a great deal of information in a minimum amount of space. Now, follow these instructions:

1. List your name, address, and phone number. (College students: Include your campus and permanent address, if you have one.)

2. State your objective: Make it brief and to the point.

3. Provide a profile. This optional but useful section is the one that my clients often refer to when they say "I can't believe this is me!" or "I hadn't thought about myself before in this light!" A profile is especially good for those of you in the accounting profession who seem a bit coy about putting all your wonderful working traits on paper. Do it. It will show the employer that you are aware of these assets. In your profile, briefly describe or summarize working style, personality traits, and achievements that relate to your objective. These are the essence of what the employer may be seeking in the applicant. *Example:* Ability to work efficiently under extreme pressure and tight work schedules (see resume samples, Chapter 11).

4. State your education: degree (BA, MA), major, school, graduation date. If you're certified, make sure to include this information here.

5. Describe your professional experience or related experience. Here's the heart of your functional resume. Starting with the appropriate action word, explain what you do at your job. You'll use subheads to convey your skills (see list, "More Than 100 Action Words," at the end of this chapter.) Part of the section might look like this:

PROFESSIONAL EXPERIENCE

Operation's Management and Administration

- Oversaw two corporate headquarter operations plus 7 branches of 2 financial institutions and 1 statewide marketing consulting firm.
- Restructured the operations division resulting in ongoing efficiency and profitability.
- Generated annual budgets and forecasts working closely with the chief financial officer.
- Developed an operation's policy and procedures manual; streamlined and improved manual that consistently met all governmental rules and regulations.
- Prepared business plans for submission to regulatory agencies and board of directors.

Data Processing Management

- Developed a profit management service for a series of integrated program modules involving profit planning, budgeting, and management reports.
- Interpreted internal corporate needs and evaluated, selected, and purchased customized software and hardware.
- Supervised entire data-processing conversion project.

Remember to include any special achievements directly related to your career objective. Always focus on the strongest points that tie in to your career objective. For more details and examples, look at the functional resume samples in Chapter 11.

6. Provide your employment history. In this section, list your job title, company name, city, state, and date position started/ended in chronological order, starting with the most recent and working backward. Accounting students and volunteers returning to the work force may not have a job title. (I'll show you what to do about that in Chapters 3 and 5.) If your job title is nondescript or if you didn't have a job title, give yourself credit where credit is due. Be descriptive: When selecting an appropriate job title that best encapsulates what you do, remember that many businesses have different titles for what is essentially the same job. For example, you might be called a senior accountant where you work, but your job may include more managerial duties than the title implies. Another firm might call that same job controller.

ORGANIZING THE EXPERIENCE SECTION IN A FUNCTIONAL RESUME

What you do in one part of the resume can help you flesh out other sections. This is especially the case for the Professional Experience section. I suggest that you first list your Employment or Work History before becoming more specific. Even though this information will appear at the bottom of your resume, you'll gain a better perspective on what you're going to write about.

What you include under Professional Experience essentially will be a description of your achievements and what you've done, taken directly from Employment History. Always focus the entire experience section on your career objective.

At this stage, you can afford to be expansive. Brainstorm your ideas. There really is no limit to the categories you can create. Start with an action word describing your experiences. After you've listed your achievements and experiences directly related to your career objective, sort out your ideas. Then, create subtitles that fit the description of your career objective and categorize the experiences by listing them under the appropriate subheading. *Example:* As a Financial Accounts Manager, you probably would have gained valuable skills in Research Analysis and Evaluation; Management and Administration; and Investor Relations.

Such labels can become the categories under Professional Experience that you will then expand with details of your work background.

With this procedure, you're accomplishing two things: First, you're describing in concrete form the many (and often unstated) ways you work. Second, you're highlighting the skills the interviewer will be looking for.

Now that you have those skills and/or areas of expertise listed as categories under Professional Experience, you can then use them as subheadings. If, as in the preceding example, you have a subheading "Financial Accounts Manager," you now describe the details of that role. For example:

Research Analysis and Evaluation

- Analyzed and researched investment instruments including stocks, bonds, insurance, mutual funds, CDs.
- Researched market conditions affecting clients' and future financial strategies.
- Developed a sharply defined, critical mode of evaluating client's needs and analyzing investment instruments and strategies.

Management and Administration

- Supervised staff to ensure accuracy of the pricing, billing, and inventory control systems for a Fortune 500 corporation.
- Led the conversion and update of a more efficient computerized inventory and distribution system.
- Trained, supervised, and reviewed financial operations staff.

Investor Relations

- Functioned as main source of daily information for investors and financial analysts.

- Served as liaison between treasury department, transfer agents, and trustees of a Fortune 500 corporation.
- Delivered effective presentations on various financial disclosure issues to in-house functional managers, in conjunction with upcoming press releases.

As you create your functional resume, visualize the employer receiving your final version. Remember, you're aiming for that interview; keep your resume on that target; keep your achievements and experience related to your career objective.

PREPARING THE COMBINATION RESUME

The combination resume allows the job seeker to highlight a specific job or selected jobs and still list other work experience or employment history. It's a combination of the chronological and functional resume. For example, I designed a combination resume for a client whose objective was to relocate and find a job as a Chief Financial Officer for a Fortune 500 corporation. He is the Chief Executive Officer for another Fortune 500 corporation with six years' experience in his current position. His prior experience included two years as a Treasurer and 10 years' experience as a manager with six years' experience as an accountant for a public accounting firm. So, we highlighted his current and most recent employment experience as Treasurer and Chief Executive Officer at the Fortune 500 corporation and listed his employment history at the previous public accounting firm in the combination resume style. This format works well for those with the following background:

1. You've had specific job(s) directly related to your objective.
2. Each position involves a completely different job description.
3. You also have had related jobs that are important to mention because they are indirectly related to your current objective.
4. If you're a student, items one and two apply to your background, and you have jobs you'd like to mention just to show your stable work history.

For some of you, certain jobs you've had deserve more emphasis than others. A combination resume brings attention to the jobs most directly related to your career objective.

A variation on the chronological and functional formats, the combination resume, by using the chronological style, highlights the jobs that tie in to your objective. Then it lists your other employment in the functional format. The combination format provides an extensive job description for a specific job or jobs and then lists your previous employment history in a different section.

To create a combination resume, begin by following the instructions for the chronological resume but under the Professional Experience section highlight selected job(s) that relate directly to your job objective (see Numbers 1–5 in the section "Preparing the Chronological Resume"). In addition, you will create a section for your previous jobs titled Previous Employment History and list them at the end of your resume. List your job title, organization name, city, state, and date position started/ended for the rest of your jobs in chronological order starting with the most recent and working backward as in the functional resume (see resume samples in Chapter 11).

NOTE: IF YOU'VE HAD NUMEROUS JOBS OVER THE YEARS, YOU DON'T *HAVE* TO LIST THEM ALL.

OPTIONAL RESUME HEADINGS

All resumes incorporate some flexibility. You may list some of the following skills or activities under the Profession Profile section or create titles for anything that is pertinent to your career objective and is important to you, such as:

Presentations
Public Speaking
Special Training
Computer Hardware/Software
Computer Language Skills
Publications
Volunteer Work
Academic Achievements
Affiliations
Leadership Skills
Other Pertinent Information
Foreign Language Skills

LIST OF MORE THAN 100 ACTION WORDS

act as	enact	persuade
active in	establish	plan
administer	evaluate	prepare
allocate	examine	present
analyze	execute	process
approve	follow-up	produce
articulate	forecast	promote
assimilate	formulate	proofread
assist	forward	propose
assure	function	provide
augment	generate	recommend
balance	guided	recruit
built	identify	refer
chair	implement	repair
coach	improve	report
collect	initiate	represent
communicate	install	research
compute	institute	resolve
conceptualize	instruct	restructure
consolidate	integrate	review
consult	interface	revise
contribute	interpret	schedule
control	interview	screen
coordinate	launch	secure
correct	lead	select
correspond	lecture	serve
counsel	liaison	set up
create	locate	specify
delegate	maintain	stimulate
demonstrate	manage	strengthen
design	market	summarize
determine	mediate	supervise
develop	monitor	supply
direct	motivate	systematize
distribute	operate	tabulate
document	optimize	test
draft	organize	train
edit	oversee	upgrade
effect	perform	

3

Accountants and Financial Professionals Making a Lateral Move and Changing Careers

MAKING A LATERAL MOVE

If you are making a lateral move to another organization or department but essentially staying in the same field, use the functional style, which will emphasize your job skills (see Chapter 2 for directions to create your resume).

In all cases, focus on your career objective. Highlight all the training you received and the duties you're currently responsible for. Sample resumes of accountants and financial professionals making a lateral career change appear at the end of this chapter.

CHANGING CAREERS

In the past, employees tended to stay with one employer for longer periods of time, even for whole careers. People also remained in the same field for the most part. But these days, many of us begin in our 20s in one field, move over to another area of work in our 30s, and again switch gears in our 40s. A former certified public accountant may take a position as an accounting educator, financial planner, or financial business consultant. A financial manager may become a human resources director or hospital administrator.

This fluidity of professional development calls for a functional resume that will focus on your skills, not just your employment history. You may be a finance manager aiming for a change as a data-processing manager, and embedded in your past are skills and strengths (from purchasing and setting up a sophisticated animated office system) that apply to that new career objective. Excited by doing this project, you decided you'd like to become a data-processing manager and consultant. Now, how do you best present yourself?

Using a functional resume format, you'll create the heading "Related Experience." For example:

Systems Analyst/Programmer

- Developed new software to implement a sophisticated customized multifunctional accounting package for a Fortune 500 corporation.
- Established and initiated implementation of training programs and seminars for new computerized accounting and database management programs.

Accounting Manager

- Wrote a business plan to develop a new computer that qualified the company for a government grant for industries impacted by imports.
- Motivated research and development staff to perform in a turnaround situation at below their earning capabilities.
- Successfully settled all lawsuits and negotiated with creditors in discounting payables and deferring payments.
- Generated a positive cash flow by reducing overhead costs, accelerating collections, and converting excess inventory and assets into cash.
- Improved relations with dealers and used their input to formulate company's plans for developing a market-oriented product.
- Prepared payroll, sales, property tax forms; analyzed and prepared financial statements.
- Assisted with inventory control and asset counts; updated product costs and budget variances.

What can often lead to a career change is the discovery about yourself that you make when you pursue a new hobby, take a class, or help a friend or family member on a special project. These are more than "hidden" skills; they are true indicators of your interest that translate so well into the essence of a functional resume.

Many career opportunities await the accountant wanting to change professions. For example, the Tax Accountant who has demonstrated leadership skills and experience in insurance, employee benefits, and pension plans could become a Human Resources Director or an Insurance Sales Manager. The hospital Controller has experience working with the Board of Directors that could lead to the Hospital Administrator position. An accountant specializing in stocks and bonds may choose to change careers and become a Financial Planner or Stockbroker. An accountant with computer programming experience may have the desire to become a Management Business Consultant who helps businesses set up customized accounting and database software to meet specific company needs. Another accountant may choose to become a Teacher or Professor of Accounting or Business Economics. Many doors are open to the person who wants to use an accountant background to change careers. The following job descriptions from resumes represent some of the careers that benefit from an accountant or financial professional background.

Fact: To become a professor of accounting at a four-year university, you must have a doctorate. With a master's degree you may become a part-time instructor at a four-year university or at a community college system. Accountants who don't have the required degrees may teach in a private college setting.

Financial Planner

Define and organize financial plans to meet individual and small business goals and objectives. Coordinate insurance protection, cash management, and investments. Recommend financial, estate, and retirement plans for individuals and small businesses. Implement investment strategies with bonds, stocks, CDs, annuities, insurance, and trusts. Develop and organize health, long-term care, and medical supplement insurance products.

Data-Processing Manager

Interpret internal corporate needs and evaluate, select, and purchase customized software and hardware for Fortune 500 corporations. Supervise entire data-processing conversion projects. Develop computerized profit management services for a series of integrated program modules involving profit planning, budgeting, and management reports. Establish and initiate implementation of training programs and seminars for new computerized accounting and database management programs.

Trust Administrator

Manage 180 accounts with total market value of $150M; revenues of $1.4M. Accounts include Living, Testamentary, Conservatorship, Unitrusts, Agency, and Custody trusts. Launch intensive Cohen-Brown marketing techniques, including financial profiling of existing client base, branch contact, and organizing seminars. Organize highly successful in-house marketing campaigns that generate new business for the bank. Conduct a week-long training seminar on new Trust Aid procedures for our updated in-house computer system. Prepare discretionary requests and monitor investments, distributions, terminations, and sale of personal property. Serve as portfolio manager for accounts fully vested in Common Trust Funds.

Vice President—Financial Corporate Trainer

Pioneer major expansion for a financial corporation of 43 offices to 180 offices nationwide. Identify, select, and educate midlevel and senior-level executives to provide retirement planning for employees of nonprofit organizations. Develop highly successful marketing strategies and workshops for promotions and sales. Establish a modular training program for 500 Registered Benefit Specialists. Conduct motivational and educational workshops. Identify prospective clients; train personnel to enroll clients. Supervise and monitor programs on location nationwide.

Securities Analyst

Manage over 60 million dollars in tax-free debt securities. Research the bond market daily to find highest yield available. Use computerized accounting program to structure clients' maturity schedule within a 1–5-year range. Educate clients concerning company's investment philosophy. Establish good relationships with brokerage houses across the nation.

Portfolio Manager

Manage $4 billion of total-rate-of-return fixed-income portfolios; long duration, short duration, taxable, tax-exempt, sterling, individuals, nuclear decommissioning, immunization funds. Implement a highly disciplined investment process, flexible under all market conditions. In charge of active trading room and corresponding settlement operations. Maintain a sharply defined, critical mode of evaluating and analyzing fixed-income investment instruments and strategies. Trade mortgages, euros, corporates, treasuries, and municipals. Evaluate yield curves, currencies, and option-adjusted spreads, duration and convexity. Established an efficient credit research system. Organize client goals, objectives, and restrictions. Monitor client characteristics.

Securities Broker

Buy and sell stocks and bonds: corporates, treasuries, municipals. Develop and maintain portfolio management with individual investors. Maintain existing equity and client contact. Raise equity for existing book through telemarketing sales.

Account Executive

Maintain over 300 client accounts. Provide client services for quarterly financial reviews and practice management advice. Structure specific pension plan to meet client's retirement needs, game planning for annual funding of the pension plan, fee review, employee relations, consolidation of debt, and profitability monitors.

Human Resources Director

Develop and implement Human Resources Departmental Policy and Procedures training manual. Develop employee handbooks. Oversee salary administration, employee benefits, insurance, personnel policies, selection, training, performance appraisals. Review all hiring, training, supervisory decisions for personnel needs, to assure adequate staffing of over 100 branch offices. Assure uniformity of operations and compliance with bylaws and federal regulations. Maximize employee morale and productivity.

Hospital Administrator

Met corporate fiscal objectives while completing rebuilding program for eight consecutive years with an operations budget of $6.5 million. Developed excellent resident relations contributing to a positive program, major gifts, and resident satisfaction. Received awards five consecutive years for reducing Workmen's Compensation claims resulting in $40K annual savings. Established operational policies and procedures for campus—each department, performance standards for each employee position. Established excellent food service program, environmental services, and marketing program. Developed three regional offices for Corporate Planning Association. Directed capital campaigns for local and regional program to $2.5M. Expanded Good Neighbor and Free Care Endowment Funds by $950K. Developed successful marketing program for Retirement Campus leading to consistent occupancy level.

Vice President of Business Operations

Responsible for all operations of 22 plants. Developed and implemented programs to improve operations and profits for the division. Quadrupled profits. Increased sales by an average of 14 percent for five consecutive years for the entire division. Developed a sales department that averaged from $100 to over $300 weekly in new business. Improved one established plant operation for a no-profit margin to 10 percent profit margin for the first time in the history of the company. Reduced receivables average to less than 14 percent outstanding for entire division. Increased loss/abuse from less than $1/4$ percent to over 2 percent of revenue.

RETURNING TO THE WORK FORCE

Many certified public accountants are returning to the work force after taking valuable time off to raise a family or for other possible reasons. If you're interested in returning to public accounting, many states in this country require that you maintain your continuing education to retain your license.

Tip: Though many private firms will hire an accountant who has been out of the work force for many years, it is wise to keep hands-on experience during those absent years. For example, you could volunteer as treasurer for a parent-school organization or for some other nonprofit service organization, such as the Rotary Club.

The functional resume will best highlight your specialized skills to show the potential employer how well your past and present qualify you for that new career (see Chapter 2 for more detailed information).

For those of you with related volunteer experience that lacks a job title, be descriptive. Give yourself a job title that describes what you did. For example, if you were a volunteer for the PTA who did the duties of a treasurer, give yourself the job title Treasurer or Volunteer Treasurer.

The following pages show resume samples of many accountants and financial professionals who have changed careers or made lateral career changes (pages 26–28) or changed careers (pages 29–37).

LADD N. THOMPSON
309 San Antonio Drive
Petaluma, CA 94952
(707) 765-2341

Objective: Bank Manager

PROFESSIONAL PROFILE
- 20 years experience with thorough knowledge of banking rules and regulations, policies, procedures and operations.
- Received extensive training sponsored by United Bank. Involved all phases of lending/banking operations.
- Served as Military Policeman and Chaplain's Assistant in the United States Army 1967-69. One year in Vietnam, honorable discharge.
- Currently in the Certified Credit Union Executive program.
- Gained valuable personal and business contacts in the finance industry.

PROFESSIONAL EXPERIENCE
Management & Administration
- Oversee operations at six offices of the Petaluma Federal Credit Union. Assist the President/CEO in the details of operations on a daily basis.
  - Serve as source of information concerning needs of various departments.
  - Insure quantity and quality of work performance.
- Rewrote and updated a policy manual for the Board of Directors of the entire credit union.
- As a Licensed Insurance Agent, oversee Credit Union Service Organization.
- Attend Board of Director's meetings.

Business Development & Promotions
- Assist in the development of a disaster preparedness computer system.
- In charge of field of membership expansion; work closely with employee groups and organizations to insure the approval of memberships.
- Assist in developing plans for Hertz-type sales, new car dealer sales and used car "Swap Meet" sales for members.
- Spokesperson for television commercials.

Personnel/Human Resources
- Assist in administration of salary and personnel policies, selection, training and performance appraisals.
- Review personnel needs and assure adequate staffing of branch offices.
- Insure effective and timely communications between all offices.
- Standardize all operating procedures. Assure uniformity of operations and compliance with bylaws and Federal Regulations.

- More -

EDUCATION
BBA, Accounting, 1967
San Francisco State College, San Francisco CA

AA, Liberal Arts, 1965
Valley Community College, Santa Rosa, CA

CIVIC/COMMUNITY RELATIONS
- **Chairman**, FOA, Credit Union Executives Society, 1988-89
- **President**, Northern Coastal Development Corp, 1986-89
- **President**, Petaluma Chamber of Commerce, 1985-86
- **Vice President**, San Francisco United Way, 1984
- **Board Member**, San Francisco Rotary Club, 1984

EMPLOYMENT HISTORY
Operations Manager, Petaluma Federal Credit Union, Petaluma, CA	1984-present
Bank Manager, Mid State Bank, Santa Rosa, CA	1981-84
Bank Manager/Sr. Loan Officer, Santa Rosa Bank, Santa Rosa, CA	1977-81
Auditor/Loan Officer/Assistant Manager, United Bank, Chico, CA	1967-77

DOROTHY STRUTHERS
321 Terry Shores Drive
Ft. Collins, CO 80524
(303) 224-0548

OBJECTIVE
Special Agent, Group Insurance

PROFESSIONAL EXPERIENCE

SPECIAL FINANCIAL AGENT   1985-present
Farmer's Insurance, Ft. Collins, CO

- Install accounting systems and resolve system problems for offices throughout Larimer County.

- Plan and oversee incorporation of insurance program into the company's accounting system.

- Explain group insurance programs to promote sales to prospective clients and establish accounting system for insurance plan.

- Explain types of insurance coverage and accounting documentation required, serving as liaison between sales agent and client.

PROFESSIONAL AFFILIATIONS
Member, American Accounting Association

EDUCATION
MBA, Accounting, 1978
California State University, Los Angeles

BA, Accounting, 1972
University of Denver, Denver, CO

PREVIOUS EMPLOYMENT HISTORY
Senior Internal Auditor, Automobile Club of America, Denver, CO   1978-85
Internal Auditor, Prudential Insurance, Los Angeles, CA   1975-78
Junior Accountant, Prudential Insurance, Denver, CO   1972-75

CECIL J. WIRTS
145 City Park Drive
Ft. Collins, CO 80524
(303) 223-4329

OBJECTIVE
Director, Funds Development

PROFESSIONAL EXPERIENCE
DIRECTOR, FUNDS DEVELOPMENT   1985-present
Denver Museum of Natural History, Denver, CO
- Plan, organize, direct, and coordinate ongoing and special project funding programs for the museum.
- Prepare statement of planned activities and enlist support from members of institution staff and volunteer organizations.
- Develop public relations materials to enhance institution image and promote fund-raising program.
- Identify potential contributors to special project funds and supporters of institution ongoing operations through examination of past records, individual and corporate contracts, and knowledge of community.
- Plan and coordinate fund drives for special projects.
- Assign responsibilities for personal solicitation to members of staff, volunteer organizations, and governing body according to special interests.
- Organize direct mail campaign to reach other potential contributors.
- Plan and coordinate benefit events including banquets, balls, and auctions.
- Organize solicitation drives for pledges of ongoing support from individuals, corporations, and foundations.
- Encourage sponsors to contribute to special funds through endowments, trusts, donations of gifts-in-kind, or bequests, conferring with attorneys to establish methods of transferring funds to benefit both donors and museum.
- Research public and private grant agencies and foundations to identify other sources of funding for research, community service, or other projects.
- Supervise and coordinate activities of workers engaged in maintaining records of contributors and grants and prepare letters of appreciation.
- Negotiate agreements with representatives of other organizations for exchange of mailing lists, information, and cooperative programs.

PROFESSIONAL AFFILIATIONS
Member, American Accounting Association
Member, American Institute of Certified Public Accountants

- More -

EDUCATION
MBA, Business Administration, 1978
California State University, Los Angeles

BA, Accounting, 1968
University of Denver, Denver, CO

PREVIOUS EMPLOYMENT HISTORY
Assistant Director, Los Angeles Natural History Museum, Los Angeles, CA 1978-85
Assistant Treasurer, Bank of Los Angeles, Los Angeles, CA   1974-78
Treasury Operations Analyst, Denver Bank & Trust, Denver, CO   1970-74
Certified Public Accountant, Charles & Associates, Denver, CO   1968-70

LAWRENCE J. GORDON
132 Smith Street
Ft. Collins, CO 80524
(303) 224-4343

OBJECTIVE
Director of Fund-Raising for a nonprofit organization

PROFESSIONAL EXPERIENCE

DIRECTOR, FUND-RAISING   1985-present
Ft. Collins Social-Welfare Organization
- Direct and coordinate solicitation and disbursement of funds for this active community social-welfare organization.

- Establish fund-raising goals according to financial need of agency.

- Formulate policies for collecting and safeguarding contributions.

- Initiate public relations program to promote community understanding and support for organization's objectives.

- Develop schedule for disbursing solicited funds.

- Issue instructions to volunteer and paid workers regarding solicitations, public relations, and clerical duties.

PROFESSIONAL AFFILIATIONS
Member, American Accounting Association

EDUCATION
MBA, Business Administration, 1978
University of Hartford, CT

BA, Accounting, 1972
University of Denver, Denver, CO

PREVIOUS EMPLOYMENT HISTORY
Assistant Director, United Way of Hartford, Hartford, CT   1978-85
Treasury Operations Analyst, Bank of Hartford, Hartford, CT   1975-78
Financial Planner, Bank of Colorado, Denver, CO   1972-75

DAVID P. FIELDING
321 Mountain Avenue
Ft. Collins, CO 80524
(303) 224-9657

OBJECTIVE
Industrial Relations Director

PROFESSIONAL EXPERIENCE

DIRECTOR, INDUSTRIAL RELATIONS   1985-present
Bud of Colorado, Denver, CO

- Formulate policies and direct and coordinate industrial relation activities for this multimillion dollar farming corporation.

- Analyze wage and salary reports to determine competitive compensation plan.

- Study legislation, arbitration decisions, and collective bargaining contracts to assess industry trends.

- Develop policies for subordinate managers of each department including employment, compensation, labor relations, and employee services, complying with government regulations, and labor contract terms.

- Write directives advising department managers of corporate policies regarding equal employment opportunities, compensation, and employee benefits.

- Consult legal staff to ensure that policies comply with federal and state law.

- Prepare personnel forecast to project employment needs.

- Write and deliver presentation to corporate officers and government officials regarding industrial relations policies and practices.

EDUCATION
MBA, Accounting, 1978
California State University, Los Angeles

BA, Accounting, 1965
University of Denver, Denver, CO

PREVIOUS EMPLOYMENT HISTORY
Controller, Raytheon Company, Oxnard, CA   1978-85
Assistant Controller, Valley Research Center, Encino, CA   1974-78
Finance Manager, Gravenstein Orchard Ranch, Sabastopal, CA 1970-74

BRITTANY SUE LENNON
943 Mulberry Street
Ft. Collins, CO 80524
(303) 224-0498

OBJECTIVE
Letter-of-Credit Document Examiner

PROFESSIONAL EXPERIENCE
DOCUMENT EXAMINER (Letter-of-Credit)
Security International Bank, Denver, CO   1986-present

- Authorize payment on letters of credit used in international banking.

- Examine documents, including bills of lading, certificates of origin, and shipping manifests, for accuracy and completeness.

- Ensure that conditions of letters of credit are in accordance with corporate policy and international uniform custom and practice.

- Verify document computations.

- Talk with customers and recommend acceptable wording for letters of credit.

- Explain regulatory and legal implications of terms and conditions, including the United States trade restrictions.

- Instruct workers in preparing amendments to letters of credit.

- Contact foreign banks, suppliers, and other sources to obtain required documents.

- Authorize method of payment against letter of credit in accordance with client instructions.

PROFESSIONAL AFFILIATIONS
Member, American Accounting Association
Member, American Banking Association

EDUCATION
MBA, Accounting, 1978
California State University, Los Angeles

BA, Accounting, 1974
University of Denver, Denver, CO

PREVIOUS EMPLOYMENT HISTORY
Senior Credit Analyst, International Bank of America, Los Angeles, CA   1980-86
Credit Analyst Manager, Valley Bank of Los Angeles, Encino, CA   1977-80

GEOFFREY R. PETERSON
4444 Westerly Road
Goleta, CA 93117
(805) 964-1111

Objective: Hospital Administrator

PROFESSIONAL PROFILE
- Senior level executive with successful leadership pattern since 1960.
- Achievements in retirement campus administration, management and operations; corporate and business development.
- Effective fiscal operations and fund development, staff and leadership development.
- Major marketing objectives achieved for national and local programs.

PROFESSIONAL EXPERIENCE

Strategic Planning
- Campus Administrator during $15M rebuilding program for 16-acre campus, 1982-90.
- Initiated the development of retirement facility - Modesto, CA, 1967-68.
- Assisted in acquisition of major hospital for Eskaton.
- Established long-range plans for Samarkand-Annual Updates.
- Developed three regional offices for Corporate Planning Association.

Operations
- Eight consecutive years of meeting corporate fiscal objectives while completing rebuilding program, 1982-90. Operations budget is $6.5 million, 1990.
- Strong resident relations contributing to a positive program, major gifts and resident satisfaction.
- Received awards five consecutive years for reducing workers' compensation claims resulting in $30-$40K a year in savings.
- Established excellent food service program, environmental services and marketing program.
- Established operational policies and procedures for campus - each department, performance standards for each employee position.
- President, Director and CEO of two proprietary operations:
  Corporate Planning Associates and Mastercarve Products, Inc.
- President and CEO for Christian Churches of Northern California-Nevada; Associate Executive for Christian Churches of Oklahoma.

Development Program
- Directed capital campaigns for local and regional church $300K to $2.5M.
- Board of Directors for Board of Finance of Christian Church (National).
- Capital campaign Director - Eskaton American River Hospital.
- Established Samarkand Long-Range Development Program.
- Expanded Good Neighbor and Free Care Endowment Funds by $500K at Samarkand.

- More -

PROFESSIONAL EXPERIENCE (Continued)

Marketing Program
- Directed marketing program for Eskaton Corporation Data Processing, Facility Acquisition, Human Resource Services and Waste Management Systems...Local - Statewide - Nationally.
- Developed successful marketing program for Samarkand Retirement Campus leading to consistant occupancy level.

EDUCATION

Master's Degree, Business Administration
Golden Gate University, Sacramento, California
1982-in progress

Master's Degree Phillips University, Enid, Oklahoma
Graduate Seminary, 1958

Bachelor's Degree: Accounting, Chapman College
Orange, California, 1954

AFFILIATIONS

Board of Directors: (Partial)
California Association of Homes for the Aging
Pacific School of Religion - Berkeley
Chapman College - Orange
Corporate Planning Associates, Inc.
Rotary Club, Santa Barbara
Transition House - Santa Barbara
Love Yourself Foundation - Santa Barbara
Visiting Nurses Association - Modesto
YMCA - Modesto
Oklahoma Association of Christian Churches

EMPLOYMENT HISTORY

Campus Administrator, Samarkand of Santa Barbara, CA	1982-90
Administrator, Marketing Director, Eskaton Hospital, Sacramento, CA	1976-82
CEO Corporate & Business Development, Sacramento, CA	1972-76
General Accounting Manager, Eskaton, Sacramento, CA	1970-72

JOSIE ANNE FARLEY
109 Equestrian Lane
Santa Barbara, CA 93101
(805) 966-0009

Objective: Human Resources Director

PROFESSIONAL EXPERIENCE

Director of Career Planning
- Helped businesses develop tests for measuring applicants' aptitude and comprehension.
- Spoke with poise and confidence in front of large and small groups of people at Santa Barbara and Ventura county high schools and business colleges concerning career opportunities and how to prepare for them.
- Developed effective marketing strategies for advertising and recruitment for a busy personnel agency in Santa Barbara.
- Counseled/administered testing to students and professionals with career options.
- Provided information on current career opportunities available as well as books, testing and courses that were applicable to their goals.

Personnel Business Management
- Minimized personnel annual turnover rate from 85 percent to 5 percent for a medium-size law firm in Santa Barbara.
- Implemented new office procedures for smoother, more efficient operations.
  - Set up additional computer systems and an in-house general ledger.
  - Updated office policy and procedures manual.
  - Developed effective employee training manuals for new staff members.
- Supervised the entire staff of associates, paralegals, secretaries, word processors, receptionist and runners.
- Prepared accounts payable, payroll and supervised the billing.
- Prepared annual corporate returns.
- Maintained all aspects of business finances for a busy personnel service.

EDUCATION
BA Degree, Accounting, 1974
Seattle University, Seattle, WA

EMPLOYMENT HISTORY

Personnel Administrator, Anacapa Law Offices, Santa Barbara, CA		1987-present
Personnel Director, Abbott Personnel Service, Santa Barbara, CA		1979-87
Staff Accountant, Law Offices of Santa Barbara, Santa Barbara, CA		1974-78

PAULINA SPAULDING
124 Laport Avenue
Ft. Collins, CO 80524
(303) 224-0483

OBJECTIVE
Personnel Manager

PROFESSIONAL EXPERIENCE
PERSONNEL MANAGER
Prudential Insurance, Ft. Collins, CO   1985-present
- Plan and carry out policies relating to all phases of personnel activity.

- Prepare computerized budget of personnel operations.

- Recruit, interview, and select employees to fill vacant position.

- Plan and conduct new employee orientation to foster positive attitude toward corporate goals.

- Keep record of insurance coverage, pension plan, and personnel transactions.

- Investigate accidents and prepare insurance reports.

- Conduct wage survey within labor market to determine competitive wage rate.

- Prepare reports and recommend procedures to reduce absenteeism and turnover rate.

- Represent corporation for personnel-related hearings and investigation.

- Contract outside suppliers to provide employee services.

EDUCATION
MBA, Business Administration, 1985
University of Alabama at Birmingham

BA, Accounting, 1974
University of Denver, Denver, CO

PREVIOUS EMPLOYMENT HISTORY
Cost Accounting Manager, Prudential Insurance, Birmingham, AL   1982-85
Senior Cost Accountant, State Farm Insurance, Denver, CO   1978-82
Staff Cost Accountant, Insurance of Denver, Denver, CO   1974-78

4

Accountant Professionals Who Are Moving Up

The accounting profession is a fast growing and ever-demanding field. If you have obtained your degree and have passed the certified board exams, you will find there is a great demand for your services. Not only are there shortages of some positions, new positions are opening up every year. You might be in the public, management, government, internal auditing, or other area; and at some point, whether by necessity or choice, you will be ready to advance to a higher position. Regardless of the business climate—whether we're in the midst of a recession or a booming economy—an effective resume can help you reposition yourself.

You need to highlight your progress and achievements in a resume that not only will be competitive but will get results. You want to show your potential employers that you are thinking in terms of a career and not just a job.

If you feel you are not advancing as quickly as you think you deserve to, a professional resume emphasizing your work history can offer you the psychological boost you need to present yourself in the best possible light. Not only will your resume show employers your capabilities, it will also show *you* what you have done, allowing you to see yourself in a positive and focused manner aiming toward that goal.

Fact: Whether you're moving up in public, finance, private, or government accounting, the chronological resume format will best highlight the progress of your jobs and skills.

MOVING UP IN PUBLIC ACCOUNTING

Public accounting firms, such as the Big Six accounting firms, specialize in accounting services for other businesses and industries. The public accounting firms' organizational structure starts with entry-level positions at the Staff level. Typically, staff-level accountants have up to three years of experience. The functional areas of operations are auditing, taxation, and management services. Level 2 is Senior staff; these professionals generally have three to six years of experience. Level 3, the first-line Manager, is critical to long-term career success within a CPA firm, since it is awarded only to those rated to have Partner potential.

Fact: Professionals at Level 3 will be evaluated not only by technical competence, but also on their leadership skills and ability to communicate, organize, motivate, and direct the efforts of others. Developing supervisory and management skills is of crucial importance to advancement beyond Level 3.*

Level 4 is Partner. Individuals in this position typically possess six or more years of experience.

Fact: The level of Partner is a coveted one since only about 2 percent of all persons entering CPA firms will reach this potential goal. The financial rewards are significant.*

Fact: The Partner normally purchases equity in the firm and, therefore, shares in all profits. Typically, a professional must be a CPA to become a Partner. In larger firms, an equivalent position of Principal is available to deserving specialists who are non-CPAs.*

Level 5, the highest level attained in a public accounting firm, is Senior Partner or Partner in Charge. The achievement of Senior Partner is obtained as a result of longevity with a firm and expert handling of instrumental accounts.

*From Source Finance®, Denver, CO.

Fact: The title of Senior Partner may also be attained by participating as a member of the Executive Committee which is responsible for developing the firm's policies, planning activities, or providing day-to-day management and administration of one or more branch offices or regions.*

MOVING UP IN PRIVATE ACCOUNTING

Private accounting firms are most of the private sector industries including the Fortune 500 corporations. Individuals in Staff-level positions typically have up to three years of experience. Functional areas of operations are Internal Auditing, Tax Accounting, General Accounting, and Cost Accounting. Level 2, the Senior category of staff responsibility, typically requires three to six years of experience. Level 3 consists of first-line Manager with six or more years of experience. Level 4 is Assistant Controller. And, Level 5 in private accounting is the Controller, who functions as the Chief Accounting Executive (CAE).

MOVING UP IN FINANCE ACCOUNTING

Finance Accountants are found in financial institutions such as mortgage companies, securities, banks, and savings and loans. The Finance industry typically starts financial professionals at the Staff level, where they gain up to three years of experience. The Finance functional areas of operation are Credit Analyst, Financial Planner/ Analyst, Cash Management, and Treasury Operations Analyst. Level 2, the Senior category, typically represents three to six years of experience. Level 3 consists of first-line Manager with six or more years of experience. Level 4 is Treasurer. Level 5, the highest level in the organizational structure of Finance, is the Chief Financial Officer (CFO) or Vice President—Finance.

Fact: Due to buy-outs and consolidations of financial institutions there were over 55,000 professional banking employees including lending officers, operational officers, and administration seeking employment in 1992. Because the economy has slowed down there is little expansion in the finance industry—therefore marketing yourself with a good resume is

*From Source Finance®, Denver, CO.

necessary now more than ever. You must have a degree to move up into management in the finance accounting industry as a result of this keen competition.

FEDERAL GOVERNMENT ACCOUNTANTS MOVING UP

The federal government has several series of positions for the accountant. Each series offers different Grade Levels. Most accountants start at Grade Level 5 and can be promoted up to Grade Level 15. Each series might have different requirements. For example, the Accounting Series requires 24 hours of professional accounting for an entry-level position. Other series are the Accountant or Auditing Series, Budget Analyst Series, Financial Management Series, Internal Revenue Service Series, and Financial Instructor Series.

Fact: If you are interested in finding an accounting job with the federal government and have a computer with a modem, call (912) 471-3771. This phone number provides the caller with all the jobs available through the federal government's Bulletin Board of Jobs. If you would like to telephone direct, call (912) 757-3000 for information on jobs available in the federal government.

ACCOUNTANTS MOVING UP IN LOCAL AND STATE GOVERNMENT

Accounting jobs in the local or county government sector will vary from one county to another. The following is an example of our local county structure in Ft. Collins, Colorado, a town of about 100,000 people. Generally speaking, accountants work in several different departments: Level 1 in the Finance Department is Staff Accountant; Level 2 is Senior Accountant; Level 3 is Controller; Level 4 is Director of Financial Administration. The Budget Manager and Budget Analyst work in the Budget Department. The Treasurer's Office employs Staff Accountants, Senior Accountants, and the Elected Treasurer. Larger county governments have Internal Audit Staff members.

Moving up in state government will vary from state to state. The state offers Financial Services Classification Series with many different positions for accountants. Many of the Classification Series have levels to move up to and others are single classifications. The Classification Series include Auditor, EDP Auditor, Accountant,

Controller, Employment Tax Auditor, Financial/Credit Examiner, Insurance Analyst, Insurance Rate Examiner, Investment Officer, Policy/Budget Analyst, Public Utilities Financial Analyst, Public Utilities Rate Revenue Agent, Tax Examiner, Revenue Agent Group Supervisor, Assistant Tax Supervisor, Tax Conferee, Tax Liability Specialist, Securities Examiner, Tax Appraiser, State Tax Specialist, Tax Fraud Special Agent, Out-of-State Revenue Agent.

For more detailed information on finding a job with local, state, and federal government in the United States, Canada, and overseas, read the *Government Job Finder,* by Daniel Lauber. To obtain a copy, write 7215 Oak Avenue, River Forest, IL 60305-1935, or call (800) 829-5220.

The best style for charting your experience if you are moving up is the chronological format. As I showed in Chapter 2, the chronological resume details your progress clearly by stressing your employment history. The resume sample on page 43 of a Certified Public Accountant moving up shows this format.

KERRY ANN RUSSMAN, C.P.A.
23501 Brody Street
San Francisco, CA 94125
(415) 967-1145

Objective: Certified Public Accountant

**PROFESSIONAL
EXPERIENCE**

1986-present   BARSTOW RALSTON & WILEY, San Francisco, CA
Staff Accountant
- Prepare various types of complex tax returns.
- Examine compilations, reviews and audits.
- Serve as client service representative for a number of the firm's clients.
- Increased technical knowledge in areas of taxation and accounting.
- Increased my ability to supervise staff members.
- Learned the importance of efficiency and chargeability.

1985-86   ROBERT C. BARKLEY, C.P.A., San Luis Obispo, CA
Accounting Assistant
- Prepared accounts receivable/payable, monthly statements and payroll.
- Assisted accountants in preparing financial statements for various clients.
- Developed a clear image of the accounting process and moderate exposure to computer usage.

1983-84   APPLIED SCIENCE CORPORATION, San Luis Obispo, CA
Cost Accounting Assistant
- Assisted product line controller in preparation of labor variance reports and departmental forecasts.
- Generated reports for annual audit.

EDUCATION   Golden Gate University, Summer 1990
TA 318 Federal Income Taxation for Individuals

BS Degree, Business Administration, 1986
Cal Poly State University, San Luis Obispo, CA
Concentration: Accounting

AS Degree, Business Economics, 1982
Northern Arizona University, Flagstaff, AZ

**PROFESSIONAL
ORGANIZATIONS**   American Institute of Certified Public Accountants
California Society of Certified Public Accountants

5

Resumes for Accounting Students and Recent Graduates

You can study hard in school for four years, graduate with honors, and yet when it comes time to enter the job market, the interviewer's first request is "to see a copy of your resume." A well-written resume that represents your hard earned skills and accomplishments will help you bridge the gap between college and the work world.

Some college graduates have heard so much about the importance of practical experience that they are afraid of not having enough previous employment to find a decent job. Others may feel confident their skills are adequate but fear their grade point average will keep them from being considered by the organizations they really want to work for. It is true that some of the Big Six accounting firms require recent graduates to have at least a 3.5 grade point average (GPA).

Tip: Paid summer internships are available through all the Big Six accounting firms nationwide. Be on the lookout for their representatives on campus recruitment during the fall semester. If you miss the on-campus recruitment, mail your resume to the firms that most interest you. It's during these internships that you can demonstrate your value to the organization.

What are they looking for? Hard workers with leadership skills and intellectual curiosity.

A large percentage of campus recruits from the Big Six go directly into auditing. Some of these firms start recent graduates in taxation, whereas others place them in consulting. All the Big Six accounting firms take pride in the professional education they give entry-level staff members during their first two years of employment. Do your homework. Call several firms and get information. Find out what each one has to offer.

Tip: The Big Six accounting firms offer more paid internships during tax season—January through April although some are available for the summer internships. Most of these internships are in auditing; some are in taxes; and occasionally you'll find an internship in consulting.

Tip: For those of you interested in entering the financial accounting industry it is highly recommended that you start out first with an internship or work experience for a smaller financial institution to gain knowledge. Most of them will offer valuable on-the-job training in all areas of finance accounting. Then, have a well thought out career plan to achieve your future goals and get into a training program of a larger institution.

Because most college students do not have enough experience for a chronological resume, a functional resume highlighting skills is their ticket to getting that interview. However, a student who has had several unrelated paid jobs and has also had internships and/or volunteer committee or other work experience can list those unpaid though valuable assets under "Related Experience" in the flexible combination resume.

Many college students are skilled in computers through college studies, on-the-job training, or personal experience.

Tip: Computer skills are a universal requirement among accounting and financial professionals. Basic PC skills and a working knowledge of at least one spreadsheet software are expected, even for entry-level job seekers. Along with spreadsheet skills, many companies seek professionals with Dbase or fourth generation languages such as FOCUS, EXPRESS, and IFPS.*

*From Source Finance®, Denver, CO.

STUDENTS, GRADUATES, AND THE TWO-PAGE RESUME

Most students and recent graduates should be able to create a one-page resume, but some graduates may have an abundance of related experience requiring two pages. That is all right. It is better to have a well-written and properly formatted two-page resume than a poorly written, crowded one-pager. Don't use a smaller typeface to get all the information onto one page. Such a tactic will hinder rather than improve your job chances. No employer wants to bother with a hard-to-read resume.

If you are writing a two-page resume, add the word "-More-" or "-Continued-" at the bottom of the first page. Place your name and the words "Page Two" at the top of the second page.

COLLEGE GRADUATES ENTERING THE PROFESSIONAL WORLD

Some college graduates have previous paid experience involving skills that directly relate to the jobs they're applying for. For example, during your last two years of college, you may have had a part-time job as an auditor intern; now as a graduate, you are seeking an auditing position with the same firm in another city. You would use the chronological format to detail the job experiences pointing in the direction of your future position. The chronological resume format works best in this situation because it emphasizes the jobs you have held that directly lead toward your career objective.

WHAT IF YOU HAVE NO PAID EXPERIENCE?

Many college students do not have any paid job experience that ties into their job objective. That might seem like an insurmountable barrier, for as we all know, many organizations won't hire someone until he or she has experience in the field. But how do you obtain experience if no one will hire you?

Well, don't give up. Most of my clients, even students, have some sort of related experience to write about in their resume for that upcoming job or they wouldn't be interested in applying for it. Think back over your school years. Perhaps you worked on school projects related to your job objective. Or what about those committees you've been an active member of? And don't forget volunteer work and/or internships in your field. Also include any special achievements that are directly related to your career objective.

Here's how to arrange a functional resume for a second-year student with school project and committee experience who wants to find a part-time internship at an accounting firm.

Under Education, list related classes taken, and under Related Experience, create the appropriate subheadings:

Objective

An *Accounting* internship

Education

BA, Business Economics, 1994
University of California, Santa Barbara, CA
Accounting GPA: 3.53

Related Courses: Intermediate Financial Accounting, Principles of Auditing, Cost Accounting, Individual Income Tax, Micro/Macro Economic Theory, Statistics, Microcomputer Decision Support Systems

Related Experience

Treasurer, Chi Omega Sorority

- Established, prepared, and controlled annual budget of $130,000.
- Delegated budgets to 8 executive and 15 appointed officers.
- Collected quarterly membership dues.
- Monitored daily revenues and expenses.
- Prepared quarterly accounting statements and annual federal taxes.
- Served as active participant and decision maker in biweekly sorority meetings.
- Learned to maintain budget requirements under strict deadline schedules and highly pressured situations while maintaining a positive attitude.

Research and Financial Analysis Projects

- Assisted professor and investment advisor with college projects.
- Conducted in-depth computerized research to evaluate investment portfolios.
- Researched market conditions affecting current and future financial strategies.
- Learned to build financial model development and to follow the market closely using the *Wall Street Journal.*

- Proficient on the Macintosh and IBM computer using Lotus 1-2-3 and Excel software programs.

As you can see, you certainly don't have to have paid job experience to apply this method to your situation. You can demonstrate to your potential employers, through school projects and committee experience, that you have the experience to move into paid employment. By the way, committee experience demonstrates great leadership skills, a quality that the Big Six accounting firms look for in their on-campus recruiting.

For those of you with internship experience and unrelated previous employment (fast foods, sales clerk, etc.), I recommend the combination resume format discussed in Chapter 2. You will highlight your internship or selected job(s) in a chronological format under Related Experience and place your other jobs under Employment History at the bottom of the resume using the functional format.

This method helps to solve the Catch-22 problem—an organization won't hire you unless you have experience and it seems impossible to gain experience unless you get hired. By pinpointing your projects and volunteer work, you can demonstrate to employers and to yourself that you have what it takes to obtain that valued first job.

THE FIRST-YEAR STUDENT VERSUS THE RECENT GRADUATE

Most of you soon-to-be graduates are seeking *full-time* work. But what if you're a first- or second-year student seeking a *part-time* job or internship in your field of study? Go for it! The key word here is *part-time*. To some employers, a first-year student means stability because such students often stay with the organization throughout their school years. That could mean two to four years of employment for you.

In addition to the following college student and recent graduate resume samples, you will find a cover letter in Chapter 6 for soon-to-be graduates.

BARBARA I. SHIN

Campus Address	Permanent Address
6750 El Colegio #136	213 Loretta Drive
Goleta, CA 93117	Huntington Beach, CA 92632
(805) 562-2134	(714) 964-5098

Objective: A position leading to a career in Public Accounting

EDUCATION
BA Degree, Economics, June 1993
University of California, Santa Barbara
CPA Exam: Passed 1993

RELATED EXPERIENCE
Management & Communication Skills
- In charge of training, supervising, motivating and scheduling cashier staff of 10 employees at a major department store.
- Assessed customer needs to help them make satisfactory buying decisions.
- Helped to establish the Korean Studies program at UCSB for the Korean Student Association (KSA) as part of a 20-member team.
- Conducted monthly motivational and educational volunteer staff meetings.
- Served as editor of The Lagoon, an entertainment magazine for the KSA.
- Trained, supervised, and motivated 10 counselors for Korean Youth Center.
- Scheduled daily social activities and educational field trips for campers ages 10-13.
- Located corporate sponsorships and donations throughout the Los Angeles area.

Accounting & Finance Skills
- Held responsible for budgeting and allocating funds for all the student groups at UCSB; maintained strict budget requirements of $100,000.
- Prepared computerized income statements, balance sheets, bank reconciliations, general ledgers and journals for a CPA during the busy tax season.
- Worked well under highly pressured situations with attention to detail while maintaining tight deadline schedules.
- Assisted the controller in auditing computerized payroll journals for a statewide medical systems corporation.

ACTIVITIES
Camp Director, Korean Youth Center, Los Angeles, 1988
Treasurer, UCSB Korean Student Association, 1987-88
Member, Associated Student's Finance Board, 1987-88
Tour Guide, EOP Campus Visitation Program, 1986-87

EMPLOYMENT HISTORY

Accounting Assistant, J & J Associates, CPA & Assoc, LA, CA	Spring-90/Summer-88
Office Assistant, UCSB Extension, Finance Dept, Goleta, CA	1989-90
Audit Assistant, Toshiba Medical Systems, Santa Ana, CA	Winter 1989
Payroll Assistant, American Medical Systems, Newport Bch, CA	Summer 1989
Library Assistant, UCSB Music Library, Santa Barbara, CA	1988-90
Head Cashier, Sears Roebuck, Huntington Bch, CA	Summer-87/Winter-88

RUSS T. KOLLMAN

Current Address
666 College Place
Westwood Village, CA 90024
(213) 968-1538

Permanent Address
888 Circle Drive
Costa Mesa, CA 92626
(714) 555-1111

Objective: A Summer Internship in the Finance Industry

PROFESSIONAL PROFILE

- Gained valuable experience in financial analysis, sales and management while attending college to earn degree.
- Developed strong computerized research & problem-solving skills.
- Dependable, conscientious and detail oriented.
- Member of the Investment Club at UCLA.

EDUCATION

BA Degree, Economics, Emphasis: Finance
University of California, Los Angeles, CA
Graduation: 1995

RELATED EXPERIENCE

Related Courses
Gained valuable knowledge in Corporate Finance, Financial Accounting, Calculus, Micro/Macro Economic Theory, Statistics, and Econometrics.

Research & Analysis Projects
- Assist professor/investment advisor with college projects.
  - Conduct in-depth computerized research to evaluate investment portfolios.
  - Research market conditions affecting current & future financial strategies.
- Learned to build financial model development and to follow the market closely using financial publications.
- Gained vital computer skills using the IBM PC with Lotus 1-2-3 software.

Management & Administration
- Developed marketing strategies for effective newspaper & media advertising.
- Train and supervise a staff of 20 employees, displaying strong leadership skills while maintaining a highly professional attitude.
- Successfully maintained inventory control, shipping and receiving; demonstrated the ability to work well under pressure with attention to detail.

EMPLOYMENT HISTORY

Waiter, The Harbor Yacht Club, Seattle, WA	Summer 1992
Manager, Big Sam's Restaurant, Los Angeles, CA	Summer 1991

PAULA BLACKSTONE
999 College Avenue
Santa Barbara, CA 93105
(805) 555-1111

Objective: A Certified Public Accountant position

PROFESSIONAL PROFILE
- Highly organized, dedicated with a positive attitude; team player/leader.
- Work under strict deadline schedules with attention to detail.
- Financed education with experience in computerized accounting and management.

EDUCATION
BA Degree, Business Economics, 1994
University of California, Los Angeles
CPA Examination: Results Pending

ACCOUNTING SKILLS
Profit and loss statement, balance sheet, trial balance, general ledger and supporting journals, accounts receivable, payroll, bank reconciliation, strong computerized accounting skills.

PROFESSIONAL EXPERIENCE

STRUCTURAL ACCOUNTING SYSTEMS, Los Angeles, CA   1989-1994
Financial Statements & Computer Skills
- Prepared financial statements under cash and accrual accounting methods for sole proprietorships, partnerships, S and non-profit corporations.
- Converted manual accounting systems to a computerized accounting system for clients.
- Designed custom spreadsheet programs for internal use as well as for clients.

Billing, Payroll & Client Relations
- Prepared billing and maintained accounts receivable for private water companies and homeowners' associations.
  - Learned to interpret customer's needs efficiently; solve potential problems in a diplomatic & courteous manner, under sometimes sensitive situations.
- Generated payroll checks and reports.

Management & Organizational Skills
- Reported directly to the owner of the company.
- Assisted in establishing a successful structure for a growing company.
  - Trained and supervised employees, maintaining a professional manner.
  - Helped prioritize work schedules and delegate assignments.

SHELLEY ANNE NESTERLY

Campus Address	**Permanent Address**
4265 Gayley Avenue	387 Ysidro Heights Drive
Westwood Village, CA 90024	La Jolla, CA 90032
(213) 360-3322	(619) 630-3029

Objective: An entry-level Accounting position

EDUCATION

BA Degree, Business Economics, 1994
University of California, Los Angeles
CPA Exam: Passed 1994

EXPERIENCE

Related Courses
Corporate/Individual Tax Accounting, Financial Management, Intermediate Accounting, Micro/Macroeconomic Theory, Auditing, Business Law, Statistics.

Computer Skills
Gained valuable knowledge in the IFPS Business program, Lotus 1-2-3 on the IBM PC and Excel on the Macintosh computer. Familiar with Microsoft "Word" word processing program.

Organization & Administration
• Organized and conducted business meetings for groups of 75 members.
  - Determined location sites and solicited dynamic guest speakers.
• Prepared and coordinated documentation for fraternity membership program.
• Attended weekly educational meetings for the cultural awareness program at UCLA.
• Learned to work well under pressure and consistently meet strict deadlines.

Public Relation Skills
• Met with business managers to promote sponsorships for international internships.
• In charge of public relations for the entire State of California as the External Vice President of the College Republicans.
• Demonstrated poise and confidence while speaking in front of groups of people.

HONORS/ACTIVITIES

External Vice President, College Republicans
Board of Directors, (AIESEC) Int'l Business Club
Membership Selection Chair, Sigma Nu Fraternity

EMPLOYMENT HISTORY

Hostess, Holiday Inn, Los Angeles, CA	Spring 1989-present
Customer Service Representative, San Diego Zoo, San Diego, CA	Summer 1988
Sales Associate, May Company, Los Angeles, CA	Winter 87-88

PAUL RUSSELL DRAKE
PO Box 1123
Goleta, CA 93117
(805) 964-3333

OBJECTIVE
A Financial Analyst position

EDUCATION
BA Degree, Business Economics, 1993
University of California, Santa Barbara
CPA Exam: Passed 1993

Related Courses: Organization of Industry,
Financial Accounting, Managerial Economics,
Corporate Finance, Monetary Economics, Micro/
Macroeconomics, Environmental Economics.

RELATED EXPERIENCE

SANTA BARBARA FEDERAL S&L, Santa Barbara, CA   1988-present
Accounting Intern (1990-present)
- Developed custom spreadsheet programs using Lotus 1-2-3 for finance and analysis of 100 branch offices in California.
- Analyze and research daily accrued interest reports for demand deposit accounts.
- Prepare and organize various statements for accounting staff.
- Assist accountants with outages and reconciliation projects.

Cash Reserve Specialist(1988-89)
- Reviewed customer applications and solved potential problems for 100 California branch offices.
- Prepared computerized payments to customer's cash reserve accounts.
- Answered customer account inquiries quickly and efficiently.
- Assisted branch personnel with proper cash reserve procedures.

PREVIOUS EMPLOYMENT HISTORY
Waiter, Marie Callenders, Santa Barbara, CA   1990-present
Systems Operator, Tri-Counties Regional Ctr, Santa Barbara, CA   1987-88
Document Control, Capello & Foley Law Firm, Santa Barbara, CA   1986-87

JODY SUK MOON
PO Box 2341
Goleta, CA 93117
(805) 964-2222

OBJECTIVE: **An Accounting Internship in the Finance Industry**

EDUCATION: **BA Degree, Business Economics**
University of California, Santa Barbara
Graduation: 1995

Education Abroad, Summer 1990
Yonsei University, Seoul, Korea

EXPERIENCE:

1990-91   SANTA BARBARA FEDERAL S&L, Santa Barbara, CA
Accounting Intern (1990-91)
- Developed custom spreadsheet programs using Lotus 1-2-3 for finance and analysis of 100 branch offices in California.
- Analyze, research and maintain daily accrued interest reports for demand deposit accounts.
- Prepare and organize various statements for accounting staff.
- Assist accountants with outages and reconciliation projects.

Cash Reserve Specialist (1988-89)
- Reviewed customer applications and solved potential problems for 100 California branch offices.
- Prepared and posted computerized payments to customer's cash reserve accounts.
- Answered customer account inquiries quickly and efficiently.
- Assisted branch personnel with proper cash reserve procedures.

1986-87   TRI-COUNTIES REGIONAL CENTER, Santa Barbara, CA
Systems Operator
- Maintained client information using IBM System 36.
- Prepared monthly and daily reports for hospital staff.

1985-86   CAPELLO AND FOLEY LAW FIRM, Santa Barbara, CA
Document Control Clerk
- Assisted paralegals with document preparation.

DORA S. PAGE

Campus Address
100 Picasso
Isla Vista, CA 93117
(805) 562-2145

Permanent Address
2109 Circle Drive
Fountain Valley, CA 92708
(714) 962-6514

Objective: A position leading to a career in Public Accounting

EDUCATION
BA Degree, Business Economics, June 1993
University of California, Santa Barbara
Accounting GPA: 3.7   Overall GPA: 3.5
CPA Exam: Passed 1993

RELATED EXPERIENCE

Related Courses
Intermediate Accounting...Cost Accounting..Individual Tax Accounting...
Microcomputer Decision Support Systems...Business Law...Principles of
Auditing...Micro & Macroeconomic Theory...Financial Management.

Computer Experience
• Proficient on the IBM and Macintosh computer systems.
• Familiar with IFPS and Excel spreadsheet program and Microsoft Word.

Accounting Experience
• Assisted orthopedic surgeon with financial and front desk responsibilities.
• Scheduled appointments and answered questions, dealing with patients in a highly
  professional and concerned manner.
• Prepared accounts payables and receivables accurately and efficiently.
• Assisted treasurer of a 120-member sorority house.
• Collected membership dues on a monthly basis; monitored daily revenues and expenses.
• Posted accounts payables and receivables to general ledger.
• Active participant in weekly sorority meetings.
• Tutored students at the UCSB Student Tutorial Assistance Program.
• Learned to work on multiple assignments and consistently meet strict deadlines.

HONORS/ACTIVITIES
Dean's Honor List, Fall 1987-88
Founding Member, Delta Delta Delta Sorority, UCSB
Assistant Treasurer, Delta Delta Delta Sorority, UCSB
Member, Accounting Association, UCSB
Accounting Tutor, Student Tutorial Assistant Program, UCSB

EMPLOYMENT HISTORY
Accounting Clerk, John B. Dorsey, MD, San Clemente, CA   Summers 1986-87

ALLAN J. MILLS

Campus Address
1256 Terry Point Drive
Ft. Collins, CO 80524
(303) 224-5948

Permanent Address
3905 Berkeley Lane
Los Altos, CA 94022
(415) 941-5678

OBJECTIVE
A position leading to a Public Accounting career

EDUCATION
BA, Business Economics, Accounting Emphasis, 1992
University of California, Santa Barbara, CA
Accounting GPA: 3.75   Overall GPA: 3.54
CPA Exam: Passed 1992

HONORS/ACTIVITIES
Treasurer, Phi Sigma Kappa Fraternity
Member, UCSB Accounting Association

RELATED EXPERIENCE

Bookkeeper/Property Manager   Summers 1988-92
BEC Property Management, Ft. Collins, CO
- In charge of all accounting procedures for a commercial building. Businesses include Domino's Pizza, Economy Imports, Del Cleaners and Haircutters.
- Collected rents, prepared bank deposits and paid mortgage.
- Paid utility, insurance and tax bills, charging a percentage to each tenant to cover costs.
- Evaluated profits and paid owners on a quarterly basis.
- Learned to work well with clients, tenants and all levels of management.

Treasurer
Phi Sigma Kappa Fraternity, UCSB   Fall 1989
- Organized successful fundraising event for Pledge Class of 17 members.
- Established a budget and allocated funds to pay for events.
- Hired by Alumni Association to raise money.
- Located sponsorships through the Greek community that raised over $10K as part of a group effort for LIVE, an organization that feeds the homeless.
- Learned to work on multiple projects within strict budget requirements and tight deadline schedules while maintaining a positive attitude.

Accounting Tutor   Winter 1990
UCSB Student Tutorial Assistance Program
- Distributed answer books to qualified students, answered accounting questions and routinely closed the tutorial center.

MOLLY SUZANNE BRADLEY
222 Soho Court
San Francisco, CA 94117
(415) 558-0002

Objective: An Accounting position in the Entertainment Industry

EDUCATION
BA Degree, Business Economics, December 1994
University of California, Santa Barbara
CPA Examination: Passed 1994

ACCOUNTING SKILLS
Profit and loss statements, income statements, accounts payable,
payroll, bank reconciliation, general ledgers and journals balance
sheets, trial balance, accruals, contract monitoring, computerized
accounting on Lotus 1-2-3 and Excel.

RELATED EXPERIENCE
Accounting Experience
- Process accounts payable for 18 mental health clinics throughout Santa Barbara county.
  - Order county services, equipment and supplies working with purchasing department.
  - Prepare accruals and liquidate encumbrances at fiscal year end.
  - Assist manager in balancing budget reports.
  - Developed a computerized filing system for accounts payable resulting in a quicker and more efficient process for locating vendors.
- Maintained computerized bookkeeping for clients of a small business management firm.
  - Prepared bank reconciliations, payroll and daily sales totals.

Entertainment Experience
- Host a popular weekly rock-n-roll radio program.
  - Oversee 35 rock disc jockeys; represent them in the scheduling process.
  - Serve on review committee; judge shows looking for quality, style and technical abilities.
  - Determine the weekly Top 35 Artist List and report to trade journals.
  - Add new records into radio library on a weekly basis.
- Buy the best selection of independent label tapes, CDs, records and accessories for a small upscale music store in Santa Barbara.

EMPLOYMENT HISTORY
Accounts Payable, County of Santa Barbara, (Mental Health)	1992-present
Buyer, Sound Factory Records & Tapes, Santa Barbara, CA	1990-92
Rock Disc Jockey Leader, KCSB, 91.9 FM, Santa Barbara, CA	1988-90
Bookkeeper, EKW Systems, Santa Barbara, CA	1987-88

LOUISA DOMINIQUE MARTINEZ

<u>**Current Address**</u>
4999 College Road
Goleta, CA 93117
(805) 222-0800

<u>**Permanent Address**</u>
1111 Marina Avenue
Concord, CA 94333
(222) 888-8888

OBJECTIVE
A position leading to a career in Public Accounting

EDUCATION
BA Degree, Business Economics, June 1994
University of California at Berkeley
Accounting GPA: 3.9   Overall GPA: 3.7
<u>Passed CPA Examination:</u> 1994

PROFESSIONAL PROFILE
- Highly organized, dedicated and committed to professionalism.
- Work well under pressure with attention to detail.
- Excellent written, oral, interpersonal communication skills.
- Active member of the Philanthropy Committee and Scholarship Committee.

ACCOUNTING SKILLS
Profit and loss statements...income statements...accounts payable ...payroll...bank reconciliation...general ledgers and journals... balance sheets...trial balance...strong computerized accounting. <u>Coursework</u>: Individual, Partnership & Corporate Tax Accounting... Intermediate Accounting...Micro & Macro Economic Theory...Auditing.

PROFESSIONAL EXPERIENCE
Public Accounting Assistant, <u>Gustin & Associates</u>, San Francisco   1987-present
- Maintain computerized accounts for small businesses on the IBM PC.
  - Prepare income statements, bank reconciliation, general ledgers, journals, balance sheets and trial balance, meeting demanding deadline schedules.
  - Interface with clients to analyze business needs and maintain better records.
  - Enter data on IBM System 34 computer using a custom financial software program.

Personnel Assistant, <u>Martin Corporation</u>, San Francisco, CA   Summer 1988
- Assisted management with personnel recruitment and orientation meetings.
  - Involved answering phones, filing and accurate recordkeeping on a daily basis.

Customer Service Representative, <u>San Francisco Chronicle</u>, San Francisco, CA   1984-86
- Created solutions in the customer complaint department on a daily basis.
  - Developed phone skills, expediting challenges customers presented quickly and creatively.
  - Excellent problem solver, dealing with irate customers in a professional and diplomatic manner under highly pressured situations.

KIMBERLY LYNN SAMPLES
438 Clover Lane
Huntington Beach, CA 92646
(714) 968-1123

Objective: A position leading to a career in Accounting

EDUCATION
BA Degree, Business Economics, June 1993
University of California, Santa Barbara
CPA Exam: Passed 1993

RELATED EXPERIENCE

Coursework

Financial Management...Accounting Principles & Practices...Public Finance... Statistics...Micro/Macro Economics...Management & Organizational Behavior.

Business & Finance and Computer Skills
- In charge of the finances for a sorority of 145 members.
- Established, prepared and controlled a budget of $300K.
- Delegated budgets to 24 in-house officers.
- Collected membership dues on a monthly basis.
- Monitored daily revenues and expenses.
- Prepared payroll, monthly reports and federal tax deposits.
- Active participant decision maker in weekly sorority meetings.
- Gained knowledge and skills in Lotus 1-2-3 on the IBM PC and Excel on the Macintosh computer. Familiar with Microsoft Word.
- Learned to maintain budget requirements and strict deadline schedules under highly pressured situations.

Communication Skills
- Assisted marketing coordinator in promotions and sales.
- Contacted advertising agencies and newspapers for special events.
- Sold clothing and accessories for a retail clothing store.
- Built a personal customer base through excellent sales ability, product knowledge and superior customer service.
- Designed store displays to create excitement and promote sales.
- Learned to speak effectively in front of groups of people with confidence and poise.

ACTIVITIES
Treasurer, Delta Delta Delta Sorority, 1989-90
Member, UCSB Accounting Association, 1988-89

EMPLOYMENT HISTORY

Waitress, Tale of Whale, Laguna Beach, CA	1988-present
Administrative Assistant, Penn Development, Laguna Beach	Summer 1989
Sales Associate, The Gap Clothing Company, Santa Barbara, CA	1988-89

6

The Cover Letter and the Thank-You Letter

ABOUT COVER LETTERS

Most resumes are not complete without a cover letter that introduces you and your resume to the employer. Providing essential information not in the resume, cover letters are necessary whenever you mail your resume to an employer. They can be personalized or generalized but are written specifically to go with the individual's resume. You can create an effective cover letter in three paragraphs:

1. The first paragraph states why you are writing; that is, what position you're applying for and whether you saw an advertisement or heard about the position or company through a referral or by reputation.

2. The second paragraph briefly summarizes why you feel qualified for the position. What makes you different? If adding the Professional Profile section to a resume will make an otherwise one-page resume into two pages, use it in a cover letter instead. Never use it for both or repeat verbatim what is in the resume.

3. The third paragraph, the closing statement, states where you can be reached and thanks the employer, as shown in the cover letter samples at the end of this chapter.

SAMPLE COVER LETTERS

January 2, 1994

Molly Hansen, Partner In Charge
Securities Corporation
12312 Wilshire Blvd.
Los Angeles, CA 90067

Dear Molly Hansen:

I am writing in response to your advertisement in the *Wall Street Journal* for the position of Fixed Income Portfolio Manager in Los Angeles.

I am currently a portfolio manager/trader with XYZ Fixed Income Management, a private investment counsel firm. With over nine years experience in portfolio management, I've demonstrated thorough industry knowledge and proven success. I am confident I will make a significant contribution to Securities Corporation. I am success oriented with high energy, self-motivated, and highly organized with a positive attitude.

Enclosed is my resume, which provides additional information about my education and experience. I may be reached at the address and phone number above. I will be glad to make myself available for an interview at your earliest convenience to further discuss how my qualifications could compliment your needs.

Sincerely,

Hanna Gabriel

February 12, 1994

Michael West, Director of Human Resources
Big Six Accounting Firm
123 Fifth Avenue
New York, NY 10013

Dear Michael West:

I'm seeking an entry-level position leading to an accounting career with your firm. Being aware of your excellent reputation and aggressive commitment to the financial industry, I would like to express a sincere interest in becoming a part of your accounting staff.

I will be graduating from the University of California at Santa Barbara in June 1993. While financing my education with experience in accounting and client relations, I continue to maintain a GPA of 3.59. I have excellent leadership skills, enthusiasm, and dependability with a strong desire to learn and excel. I am confident I will make a significant contribution to your staff now, and an increasingly important one in years to come.

Enclosed is my resume for more detailed information about my experience. I may be reached at the addresses and phone numbers above. I will be happy to make myself available for an interview at any time to discuss how my qualifications would be consistent with your needs. Thank you for your time and consideration.

Sincerely,

Charles Ladd Ryland

ABOUT THANK-YOU LETTERS

Send a thank-you letter after you've had an interview for a position you're interested in, preferably mailing it on the day of the interview. The letter should be brief and personalized. Follow this three-paragraph procedure:

1. In the opening paragraph, thank the interviewer reemphasizing your interest in the position.
2. The second paragraph reminds the employer why you are a good candidate for the position. Mention something specific from the interview.
3. The closing paragraph again expresses appreciation for the interview and states that you look forward to hearing from the interviewer.

Sending a thank-you letter after the interview will reinforce in the interviewer's mind just how serious and enthusiastic you are about the position. That very act can separate you from the other applicants, giving you the extra something that leads to your being hired. See the following thank-you letter sample.

SAMPLE THANK-YOU LETTER

January 5, 1994

Dear Mr. Grammacy:

Thank you for spending so much time with me yesterday. I am very excited about the prospect of seeking a staff Internal Auditor position with ABC Finance.

After spending the majority of my time working on a part-time basis for a large financial corporation, I am eager to start working full time. I thrive on working in a fast-paced and competitive environment and can assure you I am ready for intense work and will work hard until the job is finished and completed correctly.

To reiterate, I'd like to let you know that I am impressed with ABC Finance and would like to express my sincere interest in joining your accounting staff. If you have any further questions, feel free to call me at any time.

Sincerely,

Lucus Johnson

7

Job Trends in
the 1990s

According to the *Bureau of Labor Statistics Occupational Outlook Handbook*, published by the U.S. Department of Labor, accountants and auditors held about 985,000 jobs in 1990. Employment of accountants and auditors is expected to grow faster than the average for all occupations through the year 2005, reflecting the key management role of these workers in all types of organizations. Although increased demand will generate many new jobs, most openings will result from the need to replace workers who leave the occupation or retire. While accountants and auditors tend to leave the profession at a lower rate than members of most other occupations, total replacement needs will be high because the occupation is quite large.

Fact:　The globalization of the business community and general movement toward interdependent markets have opened new doors for international accounting and financial professionals. There is a growing demand for bilingual professionals with tax, audit, or consulting experience who understand worldwide financial issues. This is especially true due to the creation of the European Common Market and the continued growth of trade with countries on the Pacific Rim.*

Many employers prefer graduates with a broad background of education and experience. Computers now perform many accounting

*From Source Finance®, Denver, CO.

functions, allowing accountants and auditors to incorporate and analyze more information. This increasingly complex work requires greater knowledge of more specialized areas, such as international business, current legislation, and computer systems.

Opportunities are expected to be favorable for college graduates seeking accounting and auditing jobs. Certified public accountants (CPAs) should have a wider range of job opportunities than other accountants. Competition for jobs with prestigious accounting firms will remain keen: A master's degree in accounting will be a great asset. Nevertheless, opportunities for accountants without a college degree will still be available, mainly in small businesses and accounting and tax preparation firms. The increasing use of computers in business should stimulate the demand for accountants and auditors familiar with computerized operations.

Accountants rarely lose their jobs when other workers are laid off during hard economic times. Financial information must be developed and tax reports prepared regardless of the state of the economy.

The number of women entering accounting and finance is growing steadily. This trend is prevalent in small, mid-size, and large companies across the country. In the past, surveys have shown that women had greater opportunities for promotion in the private industry sector. Several opportunities for growth will emerge for women in the 1990s—many will achieve positions at the management level.

Tip: Many entrepreneurs are starting up their own small computerized businesses in the 1990s, often working out of the home. These businesses will need good accountants.

Many accountant entrepreneurs will be interested in starting a home-based computerized accounting service business.

Tip: Accounting entrepreneurs will need a resume to acquire new business. If you already have a client base, you'll want a special section on your resume for "Clients/Projects," instead of "Professional Experience." To do this, follow the instructions in Chapter 2 under "Preparing the Chronological Resume." Follow the same guidelines except under the heading "Clients/Projects," type each client's name, location, and date along with a brief description of your experience with that client.

JOB TITLES FOR PUBLIC, PRIVATE, FINANCE, AND GOVERNMENT ACCOUNTING

Public Accounting

Staff Auditor
Staff Tax Accountant
Management Services/Consulting Staff
Senior Auditor
Tax Senior
Management Services/Consulting Senior
Audit Manager
Tax Manager
Management Services/Consulting Manager
Partner
Senior Partner

Private Accounting

Staff-Internal Auditor
Staff-Tax Accountant
Staff-General Accountant
Staff-Cost Accounting
Senior-Internal Auditor
Senior-Tax Accountant
Senior-General Accountant
Senior-Cost Accountant
Internal Audit Manager
Tax Manager
General Accounting Manager
Cost Accounting Manager
Assistant Controller
Controller or Chief Accounting Executive

Finance

Staff-Credit Analyst
Staff-Financial Planner/Analyst
Staff-Cash Management
Senior-Credit Analyst

Senior-Financial Planner/Analyst
Senior-Treasury Operations Analyst
Manager-Credit Analyst
Manager-Financial Planner/Analyst
Assistant Treasurer
Treasurer
Chief Financial Officer

Government

Accounting
Auditor
EDP Auditor
Internal Revenue Agent
Budget Analyst
Financial Institution Examiner
Financial Management
Controller
Policy Budget Analyst
Tax Fraud Special Agent
Public Utility Finance Analyst
Investment Officer
Financial/Credit Examiner
Securities Examiner
Insurance Analyst
Tax Appraiser Consultant
Estate Tax Specialist

JOB TITLES FOR RELATED ACCOUNTANT PROFESSIONS

Appraiser
Budget Officer
Loan Officer
Bank Officer
Actuary
Underwriter
Tax Collector
FBI Special Agent
Securities Sales Worker

Purchasing Agent

Cost Estimator

General Manager

Certified Information Systems Auditor

Economist

Insurance Consultant

Pension Consultant

Real Estate Advisor

Securities Consultant

Chief Executive Officer

Governor

Mayor

Postmaster

Commissioner

Director

JOB DESCRIPTIONS FOR KEY ACCOUNTANT POSITIONS

Tax Accountant

Prepares federal, state, or local tax returns of individual, business establishment, or other organization. Examines accounts and records and computes taxes owed according to prescribed rates, laws, and regulations, using computer. Advises management regarding effects of business activities on taxes, and on strategies for minimizing tax liability. Ensures that establishment complies with periodic tax payment, information reporting, and other taxing authority requirements. Represents principal before taxing bodies. May devise and install tax record systems. May specialize in various aspects of tax accounting, such as tax laws applied to particular industry, or in individual, fiduciary, or partnership income tax preparation.

General Accountant

Analyzes financial information and prepares financial reports: Compiles and analyzes financial information to prepare entries to accounts, such as general ledger accounts, documenting business transactions. Analyzes financial information detailing assets, liabilities, and capital, and prepares balance sheet, profit and loss statement, and other reports to summarize current and projected company financial position, using calculator or computer. Audits contracts, orders, and vouchers, and prepares reports to substantiate individual transactions prior to settlement. May establish, modify, document, and coordinate implementation to accounting and accounting control procedures. May devise and implement manual or computer-based system for general accounting. May direct and coordinate activities of other accountants and clerical workers performing accounting and bookkeeping tasks.

Budget Accountant

Analyzes past and present financial operations and estimates future revenues and expenditures in preparing budget: Analyzes records of present and past operations, trends and costs, estimated and realized revenues, administrative commitments, and obligations incurred to project future revenues and expenses, using computer. Documents revenues and expenditures expected and submits to management. Maintains budgeting systems that provide control of expenditures to carry out activities, such as advertising and marketing, production, maintenance, or to project activities, such as construction of buildings. Advises management on matters such as effective use of resources and assumptions underlying budget forecasts. Interprets budgets to management. May also develop and install manual or computer-based budgeting system. May assist in financial analysis of legislative projects to develop capital improvement budget and be designated Program Analyst. May assist communities to develop budget and efficient use of funds and be designated Public Finance Specialist.

Cost Accountant

Conducts studies that provide detailed costs information not supplied by general accounting systems: Plans study and collects data to determine costs of business activity, such as raw material purchases, inventory, and labor. Analyzes data obtained and records results, using computer. Analyzes changes in product design, raw materials, manufacturing methods, or services provided, to determine effects on costs. Analyzes actual manufacturing costs and prepares periodic report comparing standard costs to actual production costs. Provides management with reports specifying and comparing factors affecting prices and profitability of products or services. May develop and install manual or computer-based cost accounting system. May specialize in analyzing costs relating to public utility rate schedule and be designated Rate Engineer. May specialize in appraisal and evaluation of real property or equipment for sale, acquisition, or tax purposes for public utility and be designated Valuation Engineer.

Data-Processing Auditor

Plans and conducts audits of data-processing systems and applications to safeguard assets, ensure accuracy of data, and promote operational efficiency: Establishes audit objectives and devises audit plan, following general audit plan and previous audit reports. Interviews workers and examines records to gather data, following audit plan and using computer. Analyzes data gathered to evaluate effectiveness of controls and determine accuracy of reports and efficiency and security of operations. Writes audit report to document findings and recommendations, using computer. Devises, writes, and tests computer programs required to obtain information needed for audit. Devises controls for new or modified computer application to prevent inaccurate calculations and data loss, and to ensure discovery of errors.

Property Accountant

Identifies and keeps records of company owned or leased equipment, buildings, and other property: Records description, value, location, and other pertinent information of each item. Conducts periodic inventories to keep records current and ensure that equipment is properly maintained. Distributes costs of maintenance to proper accounts. Examines records to determine that acquisition, sale, retirement, and other entries have been made. Prepares statements reflecting monthly appreciated and depreciated values. Summarizes statements on annual basis for income tax purposes. Prepares schedules for amortization of buildings and equipment. Develops and recommends property accounting methods to provide effective controls.

Systems Accountant (Accounting-System Expert)

Devises and installs special accounting systems and related procedures in establishments that cannot use standardized system: Conducts survey of operations to ascertain needs of establishment. Sets up classification of accounts and organizes accounting procedures, and machine methods support. Devises forms and prepares manuals required to guide activities of bookkeeping and clerical personnel who post data and keep records. May adapt conventional accounting and record-keeping functions to machine accounting processes and be designated Accountant, Machine Processing.

County or City Auditor

Directs activities of personnel engaged in recording deeds and similar legal instruments, keeping records of county or municipal accounts, compiling and transmitting fiscal records to appropriate state officials, preparing financial statements of county or municipal finances for publication in local newspaper, and auditing books of city or county offices and departments. May be designated according to jurisdiction as City Auditor or County Auditor. In smaller communities or counties, may personally discharge all duties of office.

Internal Auditor

Conducts audits for management to assess effectiveness of controls, accuracy of financial records, and efficiency of operations: Examines records of departments and interviews workers to ensure recording of transactions and compliance with applicable laws and regulations. Inspects accounting systems to determine their efficiency and protective value. Reviews records pertaining to material assets, such as equipment and buildings, and staff to determine degree to which they are utilized. Analyzes data obtained for evidence of deficiencies in controls, duplication of effort, extravagance, fraud, or lack of compliance with laws, government regulations, and management policies or procedures. Prepares reports of findings and recommendations for management. May conduct special studies for management such as those required to discover mechanics of detected fraud and to develop controls for fraud prevention. May audit employer business records for governmental agency to determine unemployment insurance premiums, liabilities, and employer compliance with state tax laws.

Tax Auditor

Audits financial records to determine tax liability: Reviews information gathered from taxpayer, such as material assets, income, surpluses, liabilities, and expenditures to verify net worth or reported financial status and identify potential tax issues. Analyzes issues to determine nature, scope, and direction of investigation required. Develops and evaluates evidence of taxpayer finances to determine tax liability, using knowledge of interest and discount, annuities, valuation of stocks and bonds, sinking funds, and amortization valuation of depletable assets. Prepares written explanation of findings to notify taxpayer of tax liability. Advises taxpayer of appeal rights. May conduct on-site audits at taxpayer's place of business and be designated Field Auditor. May audit individuals and small businesses through correspondence or by summoning taxpayer to branch office for interview and be designated Office Auditor. May perform legal and accounting work in examination of records, tax returns, and related documents pertaining to tax settlement of decedent's estates and be designated Tax Analyst. May review most complicated taxpayer accounts and be designated Tax Examiner.

Chief Bank Examiner

Directs investigation of financial institutions for state or federal regulatory agency to enforce laws and regulations governing establishment, operation, and solvency of financial institutions: Schedules audits according to departmental policy, availability of personnel, and financial condition of institution. Evaluates examination reports to determine action required to protect solvency of institution and interests of shareholders and depositors. Confers with financial advisors and other regulatory officials to recommend or initiate action against banks failing to comply with laws and regulations. Confers with officials of financial institutions industry to exchange views and discuss issues. Reviews application for merger, acquisition, establishment of new institution acceptance in Federal Reserve System, or other action, and evaluates results of investigations undertaken to determine whether such action is in public interest. Recommends acceptance or rejection of application on basis of findings.

Revenue Agent

Conducts independent field audits and investigations of federal income tax returns to verify or amend tax liabilities: Examines selected tax returns to determine nature and extent of audits to be performed. Analyzes accounting books and records to determine appropriateness of accounting methods employed and compliance with statutory provisions. Investigates documents, financial transactions, operation methods, industry practices and such legal instruments as vouchers, leases, contracts, and wills, to develop information regarding inclusiveness of accounting records and tax returns. Confers with taxpayer or representative to explain issues involved and applicability of pertinent tax laws and regulations. A worker who investigates and collects federal tax delinquencies is defined under Revenue Officer. Secures taxpayer's administrative or judicial conferees for appeals hearings. May participate in informal appeals hearings on contested cases from other agents. May serve as member of regional appeals board to reexamine unresolved issues in terms of relevant laws and regulations and be designated Appellate Conferee.

Auditor

Examines and analyzes accounting records to determine financial status of establishment and prepares financial reports concerning operating procedures: Reviews data regarding material assets, net worth, liabilities, capital stock, surplus, income, and expenditures. Inspects items in books of original entry to determine if accepted accounting procedure was followed in recording transactions. Counts cash on hand, inspects notes receivable and payable, negotiable securities, and canceled checks. Verifies journal and ledger entries of cash and check payments, purchase, expenses, and trial balances by examining and authenticating inventory items. Prepares reports for management concerning scope of audit, financial conditions found, and source and application of funds. May make recommendations regarding improving operations and financial position of company. May supervise and coordinate activities of auditors, specializing in specific operations of establishments undergoing audit. May audit banks and financial institutions and be designated Bank Examiner. May examine company payroll and personnel records to determine workers' compensation coverage and be designated Payroll Auditor.

Controller

Directs financial activities of organization or subdivision of organization: prepares, using computer or calculator, or directs preparation of reports that summarize and forecast company business activity and financial position in areas of income, expenses, and earnings, based on past, present, and expected operations. Directs determination of depreciation rates to apply to capital assets. Establishes, or recommends to management, major economic objectives and policies for company or subdivision. May manage accounting department. May direct preparation of budgets. May prepare reports required by regulatory agencies. May advise management on desirable operational adjustments due to tax code revisions. May arrange for audits of company accounts. May advise management about property and liability insurance coverage needed. May direct financial planning, procurement, and investment of funds for organization.

Treasurer

Directs financial planning, procurement, and investment of funds for an organization: Delegates authority for receipt, disbursement, banking, protection and custody of funds, securities, and financial instruments. Analyzes financial records to forecast future financial position and budget requirements. Evaluates need for procurement of funds and investment of surplus. Advises management on investments and loans for short- and long-range financial plans. Prepares financial reports for management. Develops policies and procedures for account collections and extension of credit to customers. Signs notes of indebtedness as approved by management. May act as Controller.

Chief Financial Officer

Advises the President of the organization with respect to financial reporting, financial stability, and liquidity and financial growth. Directs and supervises the work of the Controller, Treasurer, and sometimes the Internal Auditing Manager. Other duties may include maintenance of close liaison and relationships with stockholders, financial institutions and the investment community. Frequently, the CFO is a member of the Board of Directors and/or the Executive Committee and as such contributes to overall organization planning, policy development, and implementation.

Credit Analyst

Analyzes credit information to determine risk involved in lending money to commercial customers, and prepares report of findings: Selects information, including company financial statements and balance sheet and records data on spreadsheet, using computer. Enters codes for computer program to generate ratios for evaluating commercial customer's financial status. Compares items, such as liquidity, profitability, credit history, and cash, with other companies of same industry, size, and geographic location. Analyzes such factors as income growth, quality of management, market share, potential risks of industry, and collateral appraisal. Writes offering sheet (loan application), including results of credit analysis and summary of loan request. Describes credit risk and amount of loan profit. Submits offering sheet to loan committee for decision. May visit company to collect information as part of analysis.

Director of Utility Accounts

Evaluates financial condition of electric, telephone, gas, water, and public transit utility companies to facilitate work of regulatory commissions in setting rates: Analyzes annual reports, financial statements, and other records submitted by utility companies, applying accepted accounting and statistical analysis procedures to determine current financial condition of company. Evaluates reports from commission staff members and field investigators regarding condition of company property and other factors influencing solvency and profitability of company. Prepares and presents exhibits and testifies during commission hearing on regulatory or rate adjustments. Confers with company officials to discuss financial problems and regulatory matters. Directs workers engaged in filing company financial records. May conduct specialized studies, such as cost of service, revenue requirement, and cost allocation studies for commission, or may design new rates in accordance with findings of commission and be designated a government Rate Analyst.

Budget Officer

Directs and coordinates activities of personnel responsible for formulation, monitoring, and presentation of budgets that implement program objectives of public and private organizations: Directs compilation of data based on statistical studies and analyses of past and current years to prepare budgets and to justify funds requested. Correlates appropriations for specific programs with appropriations for divisional programs and includes items for emergency funds. Reviews operating budgets periodically to analyze trends affecting budget needs. Consults with unit heads to facilitate long-term planning by ensuring adjustments reflecting program changes. Directs preparation of regular and special budget reports to interpret budget directives and to establish policies for carrying out directives. Prepares comparative analyses of operating programs by analyzing costs in relation to services performed during previous fiscal years and submits reports to director of organization with recommendations for budget revisions. Testifies regarding proposed budgets before examining and fund-granting authorities to clarify reports and gain support for estimated budget needs. Administers personnel functions of budget department, such as training, work scheduling, promotions, transfers, and performance ratings.

Director of Records Management

Plans, develops, and administers records management policies to facilitate effective and efficient handling of business records and other information: Plans development and implementation of records management policies to standardize filing, protecting, and retrieving records, reports, and other information contained on paper, microfilm, computer program, or other media. Coordinates and directs, through subordinate managers, activities of departments involved with records management analysis, reports analysis, and supporting technical, clerical micrographics, and printing services. Evaluates staff reports, utilizing knowledge of principles of records and information management, administrative processes and systems, cost control, governmental record-keeping requirements, and organizational objectives. Confers with other administrators to assure compliance with policies, procedures, and practices of records management program.

Management Analyst

Analyzes business or operating procedures to devise most efficient methods of accomplishing work. Plans study of work problems and procedures, such as organizational change, communications, information flow, integrated production methods, inventory control, or cost analysis. Gathers and organizes information on problems or procedures including present operating procedures. Analyzes data gathered, develops information and considers available solutions or alternate methods of proceeding. Organizes and documents findings of studies and prepares recommendations for implementation of new systems, procedures, or organizational changes. Confers with personnel concerned to assure smooth functioning of newly implemented systems of procedure. May install new systems and train personnel in application. May conduct operational effectiveness reviews to ensure functional or project systems are applied and functioning as designed. May develop or update functional or operational manuals outlining established methods of performing work in accordance with organization policy.

Government Budget Analyst

Analyzes current and past budgets, prepares and justifies budget requests, and allocates funds according to spending priorities in governmental service agency: Analyzes accounting records to determine financial resources required to implement program and submits recommendations for budget allocations. Recommends approval or disapproval of requests for funds. Advises staff on cost analysis and fiscal allocation.

8

Effective Job Search Techniques for Accountants and Financial Professionals

What is the best way to find a job? Networking. Contact family, friends, and other peers. Let them know you are seeking a position in the accounting industry. That will start the ball rolling. Chances are someone will know somebody who is either looking for an employee like yourself or knows of a position coming up.

Another great place to look for jobs is through trade journals. In Chapter 10, I've listed over 80 associations and trade journals in the accounting industry. You'll also find listings of thousands of associations and trade journals in the reference section of your local public library. Fortune 500 corporations, public accounting firms, and financial institutions as well as medium-size and small private industries advertise nationally in trade journals with employment opportunities from Staff Accountant to Chief Financial Officer, just to name a few. Most professions have a trade journal, book, magazine, and/or newsletter. Ask your librarian for the name of a trade journal that would cover your area of interest. *Example:* If you would like to be an Internal Auditor, you should contact the Institute of Internal Auditors, which offers several publications and has a membership of 43,000. Each journal issue lists (in its "Announcements" section on the back pages) many jobs from entry-level to high-level director positions.

Another effective job search technique is to look in the yellow pages of your local telephone directory under the type of firm that interests you. Mail your resume directly to the person in charge of the department you'd like to work in as well as the Human Resources Department. First, contact the person in charge of the department to find out if there is a position open or if an opening is likely in the near future. Express your interest in the position and add that he or she can expect to receive your resume in the next day or so. Get the correct spelling and job title of your contact person's name, and send your resume directly to that person. Always follow up with a phone call three days later, to ask if your resume arrived and if your contact would like to set up an interview. At this time, the contact person, if interested, will contact the Human Resources Department to arrange the interview. This procedure will definitely speed up your job search process. You may even find that the person in charge of your department likes certain qualities you possess that the personnel screener may not have noticed in the initial screening process of your resume.

Those of you seeking out-of-town work may follow the same job search techniques while using your local library. The Public Library has phone directories for most major cities throughout the United States.

Always check your local Sunday classified ads to see who is advertising as well. You may find a position available that interests you.

EXECUTIVE SEARCH FIRMS

Executive search firms, also known as executive recruiting or "headhunting" firms, are generally useful if you are seeking a job or position above the $40K level. These firms are retained by employers, and as such, never charge you, the applicant, a fee. What kind of positions do these firms generally "headhunt" for? Anything from college presidents and professors, to corporate middle to executive level management, chief financial officer, hospital director, you name it.

The firms act on a retainer. Usually, they structure a contract for a specified number of months in order to conduct a "search." They're paid for their time searching, whether they fill the position or not. Of course, if they do, they may earn a bonus.

A "headhunter" will probably be more beneficial to you if you are gainfully employed but are interested in seeing what's available at other organizations. In other words, you're better off being pursued than doing the pursuing. However, if your experience and income level warrant it, by all means contact one or two of these firms. They're always interested in adding to their database of quality leads.

SPECIALIZED RECRUITING FIRMS

This group covers a wide middle range of positions in the public, private, and finance industry. You definitely should contact one to three of these firms if your desired position falls under this category. Even though some of them may use the words "executive" or "search" in their name, they work strictly on a contingency basis. That is, they're paid only if they fill the position.

Here's the key in working with a contingency agency. Select one or more that specialize in your field. They will have more of the appropriate contacts because they'll be marketing themselves to their clients (the employers) as "specialists" in XYZ personnel. But be careful. If they talk about charging *you* a fee, leave. The reputable recruiting agencies are paid 100 percent by client companies.

For further information and listings of executive search firms, contact your local librarian. I found valuable books with listings of 2,000 executive search firms nationwide in the reference section of our public library. Many of these firms specialize in the accounting industry.

Source Finance®, a nationwide recruiting firm that specializes in placing accountants and financial professionals, has a network of offices across the United States as well as in Ontario, Canada. For more information contact one of the following Source Finance® offices:

UNITED STATES

Arizona
5343 N. 16th Street, No. 480
Phoenix, AZ 85016
(602) 230-0405

California
345 California Street, No. 1260
San Francisco, CA 94104
(415) 956-4740

1025 W. 190th Street, No. 165
Gardena, CA 90248
(310) 323-0900

One Park Plaza, No. 560
Irvine, CA 92714
(714) 553-8115

1290 Oakmead Parkway, No. 318
Sunnyvale, CA 94086
(408) 982-9071

15260 Ventura Boulevard,
   No. 220
Sherman Oaks, CA 91403
(818) 905-7300

Colorado
7730 East Belleview Avenue,
    No. 201
Englewood, CO 80111
(303) 773-3799

Connecticut
111 Founders Plaza, No. 1501
East Hartford, CT 06108
(203) 528-0300 x20

Florida
7205 Northwest 19th Street,
    No. 300
Miami, FL 33126
(305) 477-0500

Georgia
4170 Ashford-Dunwoody Road,
    NE, No. 475
Atlanta, GA 30319
(404) 255-4494

Illinois
150 South Wacker Drive,
    No. 400
Chicago, IL 60606
(312) 346-7000

Kansas
10300 West 103rd Street,
    No. 101
Overland Park, KS 66214
(913) 888-3054

Maryland
7 St. Paul Street, No. 1660
Baltimore, MD 21202
(410) 685-4480

Massachusetts
155 Federal Street, No. 410
Boston, MA 02110
(617) 482-7850

Michigan
Waters Building
161 Ottawa NW, No. 409D
Grand Rapids, MI 49503
(616) 459-3600

2000 Town Center, No. 350
Southfield, MA 48075
(313) 352-8860

Minnesota
150 South Fifth Street, No. 1380
Minneapolis, MN 55402
(612) 333-4300

Missouri
12312 Olive Boulevard, No. 540
St. Louis, MO 63141
(314) 434-7070

New Jersey
399 Thornall Street, 2nd Floor
Edison, NJ 08837
(908) 494-2060

15 Essex Road, No. 201
Paramus, NJ 07652
(201) 843-2777

One Gatehall Drive, No. 250
Parsippany, NJ 07054
(201) 267-6050

New York
195 Broadway, 21st Floor
New York, NY 10007
(212) 943-4210

Ohio
3867 West Market Street, No. 227
Akron, OH 44333
(216) 762-7777

525 Vine Street, No. 1070
Cincinnati, OH 45202
(513) 651-4044

1375 East Ninth Street, No. 1960
Cleveland, OH 44114
(216) 344-7500

1105 Schrock Road, No. 510
Columbus, OH 43229
(614) 846-3311

Pennsylvania

Walnut Hill Plaza
150 South Warner Road, No. 238
King of Prussia, PA 19406
(215) 964-8900

1800 John F. Kennedy Boulevard,
   No. 1510
Philadelphia, PA 19103
(215) 665-1717

Texas

6606 LBJ Freeway, No. 148
Dallas, TX 75240
(214) 387-2200

1800 West Loop South, No. 320
Houston, TX 77027
(713) 439-0280

Virginia

7918 Jones Branch Drive, No. 540
McLean, VA 22102
(703) 790-5610

Wisconsin

1233 North Mayfair Road,
   No. 202
Milwaukee, WI 53226
(414) 774-6700

CANADA

Ontario

4 Robert Speck Parkway,
   No. 1180
Mississauga, Ont. L4Z 1S1
(416) 848-3344

EMPLOYMENT AGENCIES

If you work in a less specialized area of accounting, the employment agency may very well be of help. Who uses employment agencies? Clerical workers, such as accounting clerks. Employment agencies offer permanent as well as temporary placement.

The agency offers permanent placement on a contingency basis and may charge you a percentage of its fee. This often amounts to anywhere from one-third to one-half of your first month's salary. The organization makes up the difference. Some employment agencies will charge you the full fee, which usually amounts to your first month's salary. This may seem a little unfair in that those who can least afford it pay a fee. But remember, your competition is going to be much greater.

With temporary placement, you not only can work in many different office environments but can take the time to find an organization you'd like to work for. Many employers who use temporary help often hire full-time employees through such services.

PROFESSIONAL JOB-CHANGING SERVICES

During the 1980s, a new category of professional employment service emerged—the job-changing or outplacement firm. These firms, sometimes one-person shops, go by such names as career consultants or counselors, employment or outplacement consultants, management consultants, even career or management psychologists. They will also differ widely in their services offered. Some will prepare resumes. Others will train you in effective interviewing techniques. Still others will offer personality and skills inventory testing. Some may even offer to make a few contacts for you. What you get will depend on the firm and how much you're willing to spend. Yes—they will charge you, and probably dearly, for their time.

When, if ever, should you consider using one of these firms? Realistically, when you're ready to make a real career change. In other words, you have business or professional experience, but not in the field you want to break into. Or maybe you're at a point in your career (like so many before you) where you don't know what you want to do with the rest of your life. In such an instance, the career or employment counselor could be of great help.

The term "outplacement" refers to the practice of companies that attempt to find alternative employment, usually middle- to upper-level management personnel.

TRADE AND PROFESSIONAL ASSOCIATIONS

Are you now in or ready to begin a career in a specialized area of accounting such as internal auditor, credit analyst, tax manager, cost accountant, chief financial officer, treasurer? If you are, don't overlook the importance of joining one or more trade or professional associations. These groups are valuable in two important ways:

1. *Information.* These organizations often serve as clearinghouses for inside industry information. They also publish trade journals, who's who directories, notices of various conventions, and so forth. The information you'll gain makes this a smart way of keeping up with what's happening in your chosen field.

2. *People.* Networking—the art of letting people know who you are—can often make the difference in getting the job you want or in making that upward career move. The more contacts you have, the more potential opportunities will exist for your career advancement. The adage, "It's not what

you know but who you know," has some merit when job searching.

Again, the reference desk at your local library is a wonderful source for finding the professional association just for you. I've seen books at our local library that list thousands of associations nationwide. In Chapter 10, I've listed over 80 associations for accountants and financial professionals.

If you're excited about your chosen field of endeavor and are open to relocating in the future for the right career opportunity, consider joining a professional association to help take you there.

THE BIG SIX ACCOUNTING CORPORATE HEADQUARTERS

Following are the cities and phone numbers for the corporate headquarters of the Big Six accounting firms. Each firm has offices located throughout the United States.

1. Arthur Andersen, Chicago, IL (312) 580-0033
2. Coopers & Lybrand, New York, NY (212) 536-2000
3. Deloitte & Touche, Wilton, CT (203) 761-3000
4. Ernst & Young, New York, NY (212) 773-1996
5. KPMG Peat Marwick, New York, NY (212) 909-5000
6. Price Waterhouse, Tampa, FL (813) 287-9000

FORTUNE 500 CORPORATE HEADQUARTERS

Following is an alphabetical listing by state of the Fortune 500 corporate headquarters and telephone numbers. I found it interesting to see which cities have a large number of Fortune 500 corporations. This list could also give you an idea of what the focus may be for the Big Six accounting firms in each city. Whether you're interested in working for a Fortune 500 corporation or one of the Big Six accounting firms, this list could help you determine what city you'd like to work in.

Alabama

1. Intergraph, Huntsville, AL (205) 730-2000
2. SCI Systems, Huntsville, AL (205) 882-4800
3. Vulcan Materials, Birmingham, AL (205) 877-3000

4. Russell, Alexander City, AL (205) 329-4000
5. Blount, Montgomery, AL (205) 244-4000

Arizona

1. Phelps Dodge, Phoenix, AZ (602) 234-8100
2. Magma Copper, Tucson, AZ (602) 575-5600

Arkansas

1. Tyson Foods, Springdale, AR (501) 756-4000
2. Murphy Oil, El Dorado, AR (501) 862-6411
3. Hudson Foods, Rogers, AR (501) 636-1100
4. Riceland Foods, Stuttgart, AR (501) 673-5500

California

1. Chevron, San Francisco, CA (415) 894-7700
2. Atlantic Richfield, Los Angeles, CA (213) 486-3511
3. Hewlett-Packard, Palo Alto, CA (415) 857-1501
4. Rockwell International, Seal Beach, CA (310) 797-3311
5. Occidental Petroleum, Los Angeles, CA (310) 208-8800
6. Lockheed, Calabasas, CA (818) 876-2000
7. Unocal, Los Angeles, CA (213) 977-7600
8. Apple Computer, Cupertino, CA (408) 996-1010
9. Northrop, Los Angeles, CA (310) 553-6262
10. Litton Industries, Beverly Hills, CA (310) 859-5000
11. Levi Strauss Associates, San Francisco, CA (415) 544-6000
12. Intel, Santa Clara, CA (408) 765-8080
13. Times Mirror, Los Angeles, CA (213) 237-3700
14. Sun Microsystems, Mountain View, CA (415) 960-1300
15. Teledyne, Los Angeles, CA (310) 277-3311
16. Seagate Technology, Scotts Valley, CA (408) 438-6550
17. Wickes, Santa Monica, CA (310) 452-0161
18. Avery Dennison, Pasadena, CA (818) 304-2000
19. Tandem Computers, Cupertino, CA (408) 285-6000
20. National Semiconductor, Santa Clara, CA (408) 721-5000
21. Amdahl, Sunnyvale, CA (408) 746-6000
22. Mattel, El Segundo, CA (310) 524-2000

23. Clorox, Oakland, CA (510) 271-7000
24. Connor Peripherals, San Jose, CA (408) 456-4500
25. Del Monte, San Francisco, CA (415) 442-4000
26. Fleetwood Enterprises, Riverside, CA (714) 351-3500
27. Rohr, Chula Vista, CA (619) 691-4111
28. Varian Associates, Palo Alto, CA (415) 493-4000
29. Raychem, Menlo Park, CA (415) 361-3333
30. Potlatch, San Francisco, CA (415) 576-8800
31. Advanced Micro Devises, Sunnyvale, CA (408) 732-2400
32. Magnetek, Los Angeles, CA (310) 473-6681
33. Western Digital, Irvine, CA (714) 932-5000
34. Allergan, Irvine, CA (714) 752-4500
35. Quantum, Milpitas, CA (408) 894-4000
36. Maxtor, San Jose, CA (408) 432-1700
37. Beckman Instruments, Fullerton, CA (714) 871-4848
38. Tri Valley Growers, San Francisco, CA (415) 445-1600
39. Lsi Logic, Milpitas, CA (408) 433-8000
40. Amgen, Thousand Oaks, CA (805) 499-5725
41. Ast Research, Irvine, CA (714) 727-4141
42. Applied Materials, Santa Clara, CA (408) 727-5555
43. Sun-Diamond Growers, Pleasanton, CA (510) 463-8200
44. Silicon Graphics, Mountain View, CA (415) 960-1980

Colorado

1. Total Petroleum, Denver, CO (303) 291-2000
2. Manville, Denver, CO (303) 978-2000
3. Adolph Coors, Golden, CO (303) 279-6565
4. Cyprus Minerals, Englewood, CO (303) 643-5000
5. Storage Technology, Louisville, CO (303) 673-5151
6. Newmont Mining, Denver, CO (303) 863-7414

Connecticut

1. General Electric, Fairfield, CT (203) 373-2211
2. United Technologies, Hartford, CT (203) 728-7000
3. Xerox, Stamford, CT (203) 968-3000
4. American Brands, Old Greenwich, CT (203) 698-5000

5. Union Carbide, Danbury, CT (203) 794-2000
6. Champion International, Stamford, CT (203) 358-7000
7. Pitney Bowes, Stamford, CT (203) 356-5000
8. Olin, Stamford, CT (203) 356-2000
9. Tosco, Stamford, CT (203) 977-1000
10. Stanley Works, New Britain, CT (203) 225-5111
11. Echlin, Branford, CT (203) 481-5751
12. General Signal, Stamford, CT (203) 357-8800
13. Duracell International, Bethel, CT (203) 796-4000
14. Bowater, Darien, CT (203) 656-7200
15. First Brands, Danbury, CT (203) 731-2300
16. ITT Rayonier, Stamford, CT (203) 348-7000
17. Dexter, Windsor Locks, CT (203) 627-9051
18. Perkin-Elmer, Norwalk, CT (203) 762-1000
19. UST, Greenwich, CT (203) 661-1100
20. United States Surgical, Norwalk, CT (203) 845-1000
21. UCC Investors Holding, Middlebury, CT (203) 573-2000
22. Crystal Brands, Southport, CT (203) 254-6200
23. Kaman, Bloomfield, CT (203) 243-8311
24. Hubbell, Orange, CT (203) 799-4100
25. Silgan, Stamford, CT (203) 975-7110
26. Loctite, Hartford, CT (203) 520-5000
27. Barnes Group, Briston, CT (203) 583-7070
28. American Maize-Products, Stamford, CT (203) 356-9000

Delaware

1. E.I. Du Pont de Nemours, Wilmington, DE (302) 774-1000
2. Hercules, Wilmington, DE (302) 594-5000
3. E.W. Scripps, Wilmington, DE (302) 478-4141
4. De Pont Merck Pharm., Wilmington, DE (302) 992-5000

District of Columbia

1. Washington Post, Washington, DC (202) 334-6000
2. Danaher, Washington, DC (202) 828-0850
3. Harman International Industries, Washington, DC (202) 393-1101

Florida

1. W.R. Grace, Boca Raton, FL (407) 362-2000
2. Harris, Melbourne, FL (407) 727-9100
3. Knight-Ridder, Miami, FL (305) 376-3800
4. Walter Industries, Tampa, FL (813) 871-4811
5. DWG, Miami Beach, FL (305) 866-7771
6. Anchor Glass Container, Tampa, FL (813) 884-0000
7. St. Joe Paper, Jacksonville, FL (904) 396-6600

Georgia

1. Coca-Cola, Atlanta, GA (404) 676-2121
2. Georgia-Pacific, Atlanta, GA (404) 521-4000
3. Coca-Cola Enterprises, Atlanta, GA (404) 676-2100
4. West Point-Pepperell, West Point, GA (404) 645-4000
5. Shaw Industries, Dalton, GA (404) 278-3812
6. National Service Indust., Atlanta, GA (404) 853-1000
7. Gold Kist, Atlanta, GA (404) 393-5000
8. Savannah Foods & Indust., Savannah, GA (912) 234-1261
9. Georgia Gulf, Atlanta, GA (404) 395-4500
10. Flowers Industries, Thomasville, GA (912) 226-9110
11. Interface, La Grange, GA (404) 882-1891

Idaho

1. Boise Cascade, Boise, ID (208) 384-6161

Illinois

1. Amoco, Chicago, IL (312) 856-6111
2. Sara Lee, Chicago, IL (312) 726-2600
3. Motorola, Schaumburg, IL (708) 576-5000
4. Caterpillar, Peoria, IL (309) 675-1000
5. Baxter International, Deerfield, IL (708) 948-2000
6. Archer-Daniels-Midland, Decatur, IL (217) 424-5200
7. Deere, Moline, IL (309) 765-8000
8. Abbott Laboratories, Abbott Park, IL (708) 937-6100
9. Quaker Oats, Chicago, IL (312) 222-7111

10. Stone Container, Chicago, IL (312) 346-6600
11. FMC, Chicago, IL (312) 861-6000
12. R.R. Donnelley & Sons, Chicago, IL (312) 326-8000
13. Navistar International, Chicago, IL (312) 836-2000
14. Inland Steel Industries, Chicago, IL (312) 346-0300
15. Whitman, Rolling Meadows, IL (708) 818-5000
16. Premark International, Deerfield, IL (708) 405-6000
17. Illinois Tool Works, Glenview, IL (708) 724-7500
18. Dean Foods, Franklin Park, IL (312) 625-6200
19. Brunswick, Skokie, IL (708) 470-4700
20. Tribune, Chicago, IL (312) 222-9100
21. Morton International, Chicago, IL (312) 807-2000
22. USG, Chicago, IL (312) 606-4000
23. Sundstrand, Rockford, IL (815) 226-6000
24. Imcera Group, Northbrook, IL (708) 564-8600
25. Fruit of the Loom, Chicago, IL (312) 876-1724
26. Nalco Chemical, Naperville, IL (708) 305-1000
27. Great Amer. Mgmt. & Inv., Chicago, IL (312) 648-5656
28. Zenith Electronics, Glenview, IL (708) 391-7000
29. Hartmarx, Chicago, IL (312) 372-6300
30. William Wrigley, Jr., Chicago, IL (312) 644-2121
31. IMC Fertilizer Group, Northbrook, IL (708) 272-9200
32. Newell, Freeport, IL (815) 235-4171
33. Pittway, Chicago, IL (312) 831-1070
34. Outboard Marine, Waukegan, IL (708) 689-6200
35. Helene Curtis Industries, Chicago, IL (312) 661-0222
36. Alberto-Culver, Melrose Park, IL (708) 450-3000
37. AM International, Chicago, IL (312) 558-1966
38. Amsted Industries, Chicago, IL (312) 645-1700
39. CF Industries, Long Grove, IL (708) 438-9500
40. Gaylord Container, Deerfield, IL (708) 405-5500
41. Molex, Lisle, IL (708) 969-4550
42. Interlake, Lisle, IL (708) 852-8800
43. Commerce Clearing House, Riverwoods, IL (708) 940-4600
44. Safety-Kleen, Elgin, IL (708) 697-8460

45. Prairie Farms Dairy, Carlinville, IL (217) 854-2547
46. Bell & Howell, Skokie, IL (708) 470-7100

Indiana

1. Eli Lilly, Indianapolis, IN (317) 276-2000
2. Cummins Engine, Columbus, IN (812) 377-5000
3. Ball, Muncie, IN (317) 747-6100
4. Central Soya, Fort Wayne, IN (219) 425-5100
5. Arvin Industries, Columbus, IN (812) 379-3000
6. Great Lakes Chemical, West Lafayette, IN (317) 497-6100
7. Hillenbrand Industries, Batesville, IN (812) 934-7000
8. Clark Equipment, South Bend, IN (219) 239-0100
9. Essex Group, Fort Wayne, IN (219) 461-4000
10. Anacomp, Indianapolis, IN (317) 844-9666
11. Kimball International, Jasper, IN (812) 482-1600

Iowa

1. Maytag, Newton, IA (515) 792-8000
2. Inspiration Resources, Sioux City, IA (712) 277-1340
3. Meredith, Des Moines, IA (515) 284-3000
4. Hon Industries, Muscatine, IA (319) 264-7100
5. Bandag, Muscatine, IA (319) 262-1400

Kansas

1. National Coop. Refinery Assn., McPherson, KS (316) 241-2340
2. Doskocil, Hutchinson, KS (316) 663-1005

Kentucky

1. Ashland Oil, Russell, KY (606) 329-3333
2. Brown-Forman, Louisville, KY (502) 585-1100

Louisiana

1. McDermott, New Orleans, LA (504) 587-4411
2. Freeport-McMoran, New Orleans, LA (504) 582-4000
3. Louisiana Land & Explor., New Orleans, LA (504) 566-6500
4. Avondale Industries, Avondale, LA (504) 436-2121

Maryland

1. Martin Marietta, Bethesda, MD (301) 897-6000
2. Black & Decker, Towson, MD (301) 583-3900
3. Crown Central Petroleum, Baltimore, MD (301) 539-7400
4. McCormick, Sparks, MD (410) 771-7301

Massachusetts

1. Digital Equipment, Maynard, MA (508) 493-5111
2. Raytheon, Lexington, MA (617) 862-6600
3. Gillette, Boston, MA (617) 421-7000
4. EG&G, Wellesley, MA (617) 237-5100
5. Wang Laboratories, Lowell, MA (508) 459-5000
6. Polaroid, Cambridge, MA (617) 577-2000
7. Cabot, Boston, MA (617) 345-0100
8. Dr Holdings Inc. of Del., Bedford, MA (617) 275-1800
9. Amoskeag, Boston, MA (617) 262-4000
10. Data General, Westboro, MA (508) 366-8911
11. Ocean Spray Cranberries, Lakeville-Middleboro, MA (508) 946-1000
12. Thermo Electron, Waltham, MA (617) 622-1000
13. Millipore, Bedford, MA (617) 275-9200
14. Stanhome, Westfield, MA (413) 562-3631
15. Analog Devices, Norwood, MA (617) 329-4700

Michigan

1. General Motors, Detroit, MI (313) 556-5000
2. Ford Motor, Dearborn, MI (313) 322-3000
3. Chrysler, Highland Park, MI (313) 956-5741
4. Dow Chemical, Midland, MI (517) 636-1000
5. Whirlpool, Benton Harbor, MI (616) 926-5000
6. Kellogg, Battle Creek, MI (616) 961-2000
7. Upjohn, Kalamazoo, MI (616) 323-4000
8. Masco, Taylor, MI (313) 274-7400
9. Dow Corning, Midland, MI (517) 496-4000
10. Masco Industries, Taylor, MI (313) 274-7400

11. Federal-Mogul, Southfield, MI (313) 354-7700
12. Gerber Products, Fremont, MI (616) 928-2000
13. Tecumseh Products, Tecumseh, MI (517) 423-8411
14. LSS Holdings, Southfield, MI (313) 746-1500
15. Holnam, Dundee, MI (313) 529-2411
16. Herman Miller, Seeland, MI (616) 772-3300
17. Thorn Apple Valley, Southfield, MI (313) 552-0700
18. SPX, Muskegon, MI (616) 724-5000
19. LA-Z-Boy Chair, Monroe, MI (313) 242-1444
20. International Controls, Kalamazoo, MI (616) 343-6121

Minnesota

1. Minnesota Mining & Manufacturing, St. Paul, MN (612) 733-1110
2. General Mills, Minneapolis, MN (612) 540-2311
3. Honeywell, Minneapolis, MN (612) 870-5200
4. George A. Hormel, Austin, MN (507) 437-5611
5. Land O'Lakes, Arden Hills, MN (612) 481-2222
6. International Multifoods, Minneapolis, MN (612) 340-3300
7. Deluxe, St. Paul, MN (612) 483-7111
8. Pentair, St. Paul, MN (612) 636-7920
9. Bemis, Minneapolis, MN (612) 376-3000
10. Alliant Techsystems, Edina, MN (612) 939-2000
11. Medtronic, Minneapolis, MN (612) 574-4000
12. Cray Research, Eagan, MN (612) 683-7100
13. Jostens, Minneapolis, MN (612) 830-3300
14. H.B. Fuller, St. Paul, MN (612) 645-3401
15. Toro, Bloomington, MN (612) 888-8801
16. Valspar, Minneapolis, MN (612) 332-7371

Mississippi

1. First Mississippi, Jackson, MS (601) 948-7550

Missouri

1. McDonnell Douglas, St. Louis, MO (314) 232-0232
2. Anheuser-Busch, St. Louis, MO (314) 577-2000

3. Monsanto, St. Louis, MO (314) 694-1000
4. Emerson Electric, St. Louis, MO (314) 553-2000
5. Ralston Purina, St. Louis, MO (314) 982-1000
6. Farmland Industries, Kansas City, MO (816) 459-6000
7. Jefferson Smurfit, St. Louis, MO (314) 746-1100
8. Mid-American Dairymen, Springfield, MO (417) 865-7100
9. Interco, St. Louis, MO (314) 863-1100
10. Interstate Bakeries, Kansas City, MO (816) 561-6600
11. Leggett & Platt, Carthage, MO (417) 358-8131
12. Kellwood, St. Louis, MO (314) 576-3100

Nebraska

1. Conagra, Omaha, NE (402) 595-4000
2. Berkshire Hathaway, Omaha, NE (402) 346-1400
3. AG Processing, Omaha, NE (402) 496-7809

New Hampshire

1. Tyco Laboratories, Exeter, NH (603) 778-9700
2. Henley Group, Hampton, NH (603) 926-5911

New Jersey

1. Johnson & Johnson, New Brunswick, NJ (908) 524-0400
2. Allied-Signal, Morristown, NJ (201) 455-2000
3. Merck, Rahway, NJ (908) 594-4000
4. Hoechst Celanese, Bridgewater, NJ (908) 231-2000
5. Campbell Soup, Camden, NJ (609) 342-4800
6. CPC International, Englewood Cliffs, NJ (201) 894-4000
7. Warner-Lambert, Morris Plains, NJ (201) 540-2000
8. American Cyanamid, Wayne, NJ (201) 831-2000
9. BASF, Parsippany, NJ (201) 397-2700
10. Schering-Plough, Madison, NJ (201) 822-7000
11. Ingersoll-Rand, Woodcliff Lake, NJ (201) 573-0123
12. Union Camp, Wayne, NJ (201) 628-2000
13. Engelhard, Iselin, NJ (908) 205-5000
14. Becton Dickinson, Franklin Lakes, NJ (201) 847-6800
15. Armco, Parsippany, NJ (201) 316-5200

16. Federal Paper Board, Montvale, NJ (201) 391-1776
17. IMO Industries, Lawrenceville, NJ (609) 896-7600
18. GAF, Wayne, NJ (201) 628-3000
19. C.R. Bard, Murray Hill, NJ (908) 277-8000
20. Wellman, Shrewsbury, NJ (908) 542-7300
21. Thomas & Betts, Bridgewater, NJ (908) 685-1600
22. Block Drug, Jersey City, NJ (201) 434-3000

New York

1. International Business Machines, Armonk, NY (914) 765-1900
2. Philip Morris, New York, NY (212) 880-5000
3. Texaco, White Plains, NY (914) 253-4000
4. Pepsico, Purchase, NY (914) 253-2000
5. Eastman Kodak, Rochester, NY (716) 724-4000
6. RJR Nabisco, Holdings, NY (212) 258-5600
7. International Paper, Purchase, NY (914) 397-1500
8. Bristol-Myers Squibb, New York, NY (212) 546-4000
9. Unilever U.S., New York, NY (212) 888-1260
10. Borden, New York, NY (212) 573-4000
11. Pfizer, New York, NY (212) 573-2323
12. Hanson Industries NA, New York, NY (212) 759-8477
13. American Home Products, New York, NY (212) 878-5000
14. Amerada Hess, New York, NY (212) 997-8500
15. Colgate Palmolive, New York, NY (212) 310-2000
16. North American Philips, New York, NY (212) 850-5000
17. Grumman, Bethpage, NY (516) 575-0574
18. Amax, New York, NY (212) 856-4200
19. J.E. Seagram, New York, NY (212) 572-7000
20. American Standard, New York, NY (212) 703-5100
21. Avon Products, New York, NY (212) 546-6015
22. Agway, De Witt, NY (315) 449-7061
23. Corning, Corning, NY (607) 974-9000
24. Quantum Chemical, New York, NY (212) 949-5000
25. Reader's Digest Association, Pleasantville, NY 914/238-1000
26. Westvaco, New York, NY (212) 688-5000
27. Dover, New York, NY (212) 922-1640

28. Sequa, New York, NY (212) 986-5500
29. Loral, New York, NY (212) 697-1105
30. Liz Claiborne, New York, NY (212) 354-4900
31. McGraw-Hill, New York, NY (212) 512-2000
32. Asarco, New York, NY (212) 510-2000
33. Dow Jones, New York, NY (212) 416-2000
34. New York Times, New York, NY (212) 556-1234
35. Witco, New York, NY (212) 605-3800
36. Bausch & Lomb, Rochester, NY (716) 338-6000
37. Coltec Industries, New York, NY (212) 940-0400
38. Crane, New York, NY (212) 415-7300
39. Brooke Group, New York, NY (212) 486-6100
40. Dresser-Rand, Corning, NY (607) 937-6400
41. Domino Sugar, New York, NY (212) 789-9700
42. International Flavors & Fragrance, New York, NY (212) 765-5500
43. Mark IV Industries, Amherst, NY (716) 689-4972
44. Leslie Fay, New York, NY (212) 221-4000
45. Phillips-Van Heusen, New York, NY (212) 541-5200
46. Gitano Group, New York, NY (212) 819-0707
47. Tambrands, White Plains, NY (914) 696-6000
48. Pall, East Hills, NY (516) 484-5400
49. Carter-Wallace, New York, NY (212) 339-5000
50. UIS, New York, NY (212) 581-7600
51. Carlisle, Syracuse, NY (315) 474-2500
52. Warnaco Group, New York, NY (212) 661-1300
53. Goulds Pumps, Seneca Falls, NY (315) 568-2811
54. Ply Gem, New York, NY (212) 832-1550
55. Albany International, Albany, NY (518) 445-2200
56. Standard Motor, New York, NY (718) 392-0200

North Carolina

1. Burlington Ind. Capital, Greensboro, NC (919) 379-2000
2. Nucor, Charlotte, NC (704) 366-7000
3. Standard Commercial, Wilson, NC (919) 291-5507

4. Cone Mills, Greensboro, NC (919) 379-6220
5. Guilford Mills, Greensboro, NC (919) 316-4000

Ohio

1. Proctor & Gamble, Cincinnati, OH (513) 983-1100
2. Goodyear Tire & Rubber, Akron, OH (216) 796-2121
3. TRW, Cleveland, OH (216) 291-7000
4. Chiquita Brands International, Cincinnati, OH (513) 784-8000
5. Dana, Toledo, OH (419) 535-4500
6. Mead, Dayton, OH (513) 495-6323
7. Owens-Illinois, Toledo, OH (419) 247-5000
8. Eaton, Cleveland, OH (216) 523-5000
9. Owens-Corning Fiberglas, Toledo, OH (419) 248-8000
10. Sherwin-Williams, Cleveland, OH (216) 566-2000
11. B.F. Goodrich, Bath, OH (216) 374-2000
12. Parker Hannifin, Cleveland, OH (216) 531-3000
13. Gencorp, Fairlawn, OH (216) 869-4200
14. Trinova, Maumee, OH (419) 867-2200
15. Rubbermaid, Wooster, OH (216) 264-6464
16. Timken, Canton, OH (216) 438-3000
17. Reliance Electric, Cleveland, OH (216) 266-5800
18. Lubrizol, Wickliffe, OH (216) 943-4200
19. American Greetings, Cleveland, OH (216) 252-7300
20. NACCO Industries, Mayfield Heights, OH (216) 449-9600
21. Figgie International, Willoughby, OH (216) 953-2700
22. M.A. Hanna, Cleveland, OH (216) 589-4000
23. Ferro, Cleveland, OH (216) 641-8580
24. Cooper Tire & Rubber, Findlay, OH (419) 423-1321
25. Worthington Industries, Columbus, OH (614) 438-3210
26. Lincoln Electric, Cleveland, OH (216) 481-1000
27. Cincinnati Milacron, Cincinnati, OH (513) 841-8100
28. A. Schulman, Akron, OH (216) 666-3751
29. Standard Register, Dayton, OH (513) 443-1000
30. Huffy, Miamisburg, OH (513) 866-6251
31. Standard Products, Cleveland, OH (216) 281-8300

32. Sealy Holdings, Cleveland, OH (216) 522-1310
33. Reynolds & Reynolds, Dayton, OH (513) 443-2000
34. Eagle-Picher Industries, Cincinnati, OH (513) 721-7010

Oklahoma

1. Phillips Petroleum, Bartlesville, OK (918) 661-6600
2. Citgo Petroleum, Tulsa, OK (918) 495-4000
3. Kerr-McGee, Oklahoma City, OK (405) 270-1313
4. Mapco, Tulsa, OK (918) 581-1800

Oregon

1. Willamette Industries, Portland, OR (503) 227-5581
2. Louisiana-Pacific, Portland, OR (503) 221-0800
3. Tektronix, Wilsonville, OR (503) 627-7111
4. Nerco, Portland, OR (503) 731-6600
5. Precision Castparts, Portland, OR (503) 777-3881

Pennsylvania

1. USX, Pittsburgh, PA (412) 433-1121
2. Westinghouse Electric, Pittsburgh, PA (412) 244-2000
3. Sun, Philadelphia, PA (215) 977-3000
4. Aluminum Company of America, Pittsburgh, PA (412) 553-4545
5. Unisys, Blue Bell, PA (215) 986-4011
6. H.J. Heinz, Pittsburgh, PA (412) 456-5700
7. Miles, Pittsburgh, PA (412) 394-5500
8. PPG Industries, Pittsburgh, PA (412) 434-3131
9. Scott Paper, Philadelphia, PA (215) 522-5000
10. Bethlehem Steel, Bethlehem, PA (215) 694-2424
11. Rhone-Poulenc Rorer, Collegeville, PA (215) 454-8000
12. Crown Cork & Seal, Philadelphia, PA (215) 698-5100
13. Amp, Harrisburg, PA (717) 564-0100
14. VF, Wyomissing, PA (215) 378-1151
15. Air Products & Chemicals, Allentown, PA (215) 481-4911
16. Hershey Foods, Hershey, PA (717) 534-4280

17. Rohm & Haas, Philadelphia, PA (215) 592-3000
18. Armstrong World Indust., Lancaster, PA (717) 397-0611
19. National Steel, Pittsburgh, PA (412) 394-4100
20. Harsco, Wormleysburg, PA (717) 763-6064
21. York International, York, PA (717) 771-7890
22. Cyclops Industries, Pittsburgh, PA (412) 343-4000
23. Allegheny Ludlum, Pittsburgh, PA (412) 394-2800
24. Quaker State, Oil City, PA (814) 676-7676
25. Exide, Reading, PA (215) 378-0500
26. Ametek, Paoli, PA (215) 647-2121
27. Betz Laboratories, Trevose, PA (215) 355-3300
28. Joy Technologies, Pittsburgh, PA (412) 562-4500
29. Robertson-Ceco, Pittsburgh, PA (412) 281-3200
30. Lukens, Coatesville, PA (215) 383-2000
31. Kennametal, Latrobe, PA (412) 539-5000
32. P.H. Glatfelter, Spring Grove, PA (717) 225-4711
33. Westmoreland Coal, Philadelphia, PA (215) 545-2500
34. Carpenter Technology, Reading, PA (215) 371-2000

Rhode Island

1. Textron, Providence, RI (401) 421-2800
2. Hasbro, Pawtucket, RI (401) 431-8697
3. Nortek, Providence, RI (401) 751-1600
4. Sunbeam/Oster, Providence, RI (401) 831-0050

South Carolina

1. Springs Industries, Fort Mill, SC (803) 547-1500
2. Sonoco Products, Hartsville, SC (803) 383-7000
3. JPS Textile Group, Greenville, SC (803) 239-3900
4. Delta Woodside Industries, Greenville, SC (803) 232-8301

Tennessee

1. Arcadian, Memphis, TN (901) 758-5200
2. Constar International, Chattanooga, TN (615) 267-2973

Texas

1. Exxon, Irving, TX (214) 444-1000
2. Shell Oil, Houston, TX (713) 241-6161
3. Tenneco, Houston, TX (713) 757-2131
4. Coastal, Houston, TX (713) 877-1400
5. Kimberly-Clark, Dallas, TX (214) 830-1200
6. Texas Instruments, Dallas, TX (214) 995-2551
7. Cooper Industries, Houston, TX (713) 739-5400
8. LTV, Dallas, TX (214) 979-7711
9. Lyondell Petrochemical, Houston, TX (713) 652-7200
10. Dresser Industries, Dallas, TX (214) 740-6000
11. Fina, Dallas, TX (214) 750-2400
12. Compaq Computer, Houston, TX (713) 370-0670
13. Baker Hughes, Houston, TX (713) 439-8600
14. Pennzoil, Houston, TX (713) 546-4000
15. Diamond Shamrock, San Antonio, TX (512) 641-6800
16. Temple-Inland, Diboll, TX (409) 829-5511
17. Maxxam, Houston, TX (713) 975-7600
18. E-Systems, Dallas, TX (214) 661-1000
19. Oryx Energy, Dallas, TX (214) 715-4000
20. Trinity Industries, Dallas, TX (214) 631-4420
21. Tesoro Petroleum, San Antonio, TX (512) 828-8484
22. Union Texas Petroleum, Houston, TX (713) 623-6544
23. Valero Energy, San Antonio, TX (512) 246-2000
24. NL Industries, Houston, TX (713) 987-5000
25. Maxus Energy, Dallas, TX (214) 953-2000
26. Mitchell Energy & Development, The Woodlands, TX (713) 377-5500
27. Pilgrim's Pride, Pittsburg, TX (903) 856-7901
28. Valhi, Dallas, TX (214) 233-1700
29. Imperial Holly, Sugar Land, TX (713) 491-9181
30. Baroid, Houston, TX (713) 987-5000
31. Vista Chemical, Houston, TX (713) 588-3000
32. Insilco, Midland, TX (915) 684-4411
33. NCH, Irving, TX (214) 438-0251

34. Texas Industries, Dallas, TX (214) 647-6700
35. Stewart & Stevenson Service, Houston, TX (713) 868-7700
36. Dr. Pepper/Seven-Up, Dallas, TX (214) 360-7000
37. Quanex, Houston, TX (713) 961-4600
38. Dell Computer, Austin, TX (512) 338-4400
39. Sterling Chemicals, Houston, TX (713) 650-3700

Utah

1. Thiokol, Ogden, UT (801) 629-2270

Virginia

1. Mobil, Fairfax, VA (703) 846-3000
2. General Dynamics, Falls Church, VA (703) 876-3000
3. Reynolds Metals, Richmond, VA (804) 281-2000
4. James River Corp. of VA., Richmond, VA (804) 644-5411
5. Gannett, Arlington, VA (703) 284-6000
6. Universal, Richmond, VA (804) 359-9311
7. Ethyl, Richmond, VA (804) 788-5000
8. LaFarge, Reston, VA (703) 264-3600
9. Smithfield Foods, Smithfield, VA (804) 357-4321
10. Dibrell Brothers, Danville, VA (804) 792-7511
11. Chesapeake, Richmond, VA (804) 697-1000
12. Fairchild, Chantilly, VA (703) 478-5800
13. Media General, Richmond, VA (804) 649-6000

Washington

1. Boeing, Seattle, WA (206) 655-2121
2. Weyerhaeuser, Tacoma, WA (206) 924-2345
3. Paccar, Bellevue, WA (206) 455-7400
4. Burlington Resources, Seattle, WA (206) 467-3838
5. Longview Fibre, Longview, WA (206) 425-1550

West Virginia

1. Weirton Steel, Weirton, WV (304) 797-2000
2. Wheeling-Pittsburgh, Wheeling, WV (304) 234-2400

Wisconsin

1. Johnson Controls, Milwaukee, WI (414) 228-1200
2. Harnischfeger Industries, Brookfield, WI (414) 671-4400
3. Fort Howard, Green Bay, WI (414) 435-8821
4. Briggs & Stratton, Wauwatosa, WI (414) 259-5333
5. Harley-Davidson, Milwaukee, WI (414) 342-4680
6. A.O. Smith, Milwaukee, WI (414) 359-4000
7. Snap-On Tools, Kenosha, WI (414) 656-5200
8. Consolidated Papers, Wisconsin Rapids, WI (715) 422-3111
9. Universal Foods, Milwaukee, WI (414) 271-6755
10. Terex, Green Bay, WI (414) 435-5322
11. Banta, Menasha, WI (414) 722-7777
12. Wisconsin Dairies Coop., Baraboo, WI (608) 356-8316

9

Preparing for the Interview in the Accounting Profession

Interviews can be both nerve-racking and exciting. Following these suggestions can greatly reduce your tension level.

1. Call the firm or corporation beforehand and request information. Later, when an interviewer asks if you are familiar with the organization, you can make a positive impression by mentioning various aspects of the business. A little bit of research can go a long way.

Tip: Know the corporation's or firm's purpose, product, financial position, and regional focus, if they have one. Be prepared to let the interviewer know you are aware of the corporation's needs and reputation in the industry.

You can call or write to the firm's Human Resources Department and ask for this specific information before going in for the interview.

Tip: Always schedule an appointment for an interview. Scheduling time with the recruiter demonstrates professionalism.

2. Check with the reference librarian of your public library for information about organizations that are out of town.

3. Bring three or four resumes with you to the interview in case you are interviewed by more than one decision maker. Hand a resume to each interviewer and always keep one for yourself. Chances are the interviewer will use your resume to interview you, which will make the experience much smoother for everyone. You may refer to your resume during the interview, but try to memorize its main points beforehand.

4. Always bring a pad of paper and pen to the interview. Ask questions about the job and take notes. You may want to jot down a few questions before you go on the interview. Also, write the interviewer's name and title (with the correct spelling) on your note pad so that you can address a thank-you letter after the interview.

Tip: Most recruiters will be favorably impressed if you come prepared for the interview. It demonstrates to them just how serious you are about the job.

5. Think positive! Focus on your strengths. Talk about what you do have to offer, not what you don't. If you're applying for a position you do not have experience in yet, focus on enthusiasm and eagerness to learn. Do not even think about your lack of experience. Enthusiasm is a great asset: Employers often would rather train an enthusiastic employee with no experience than hire an experienced employee who lacks that quality. Most accounting professionals already have gone through many years of specialized training. When seeking to fill a specific position, financial employers look for a trained professional who has leadership skills along with the ability to work long hours and to work well under tight deadline schedules. If you can demonstrate that you possess these qualities, you are likely to get the job.

6. That you are looking for job security is also something most employers like to hear. It confirms in their minds that you really are planning to stay with the organization for a decent amount of time. But most importantly, it provides a bond that is mutually beneficial for both parties—employer and employee.

7. After the interview, immediately send a personalized thank-you letter to the potential employer.

TOUGH QUESTIONS MOST ASKED IN THE INTERVIEW: THE ANSWERS THE INTERVIEWER WANTS TO HEAR

The employer is looking for a candidate who demonstrates professional maturity, technical skills, good character, creativity, and compatibility with the company. The following are questions and answers in these categories.

Professional Maturity

Q. How would you handle a conflict resolution with your superior?

A. Speak to my boss about it directly. If it's personal, work it out within myself.

Q. What would you do if you disagreed with a superior's decision, what actions would you take?

A. Check with the Financial Accounting Standards Board (FASB) or Commerce Clearing House (CCH) on the issue, find documentation to support my decision, and ask my superior for the same and act accordingly.

Q. Can you describe a conflict and how you would resolve it?

A. (Demonstrate flexibility skills. Be prepared to talk about a specific conflict that you were involved in where all parties were satisfied in the end.)

Technical Skills

Q. What are your greatest strengths and weaknesses?

A. My strength is the ability to communicate well with all types of people. And I meet strict deadline schedules to complete projects. I have strong computer skills. My biggest weakness is I work too hard.

Q. What was the biggest contribution you made in your current position?

A. Name any awards or recognitions you've received or large accounts you've brought into the company. (Maybe you were the key member in setting up a customized computer system that was not in your current job requirement.)

Q. How would your references rate your technical competence?

A. Ability to work on my own with very little or not assistance. Demonstrate leadership skills. Ability to motivate others.

Character

Q. Where do you see yourself in 5 years? In 10 years?

A. I see myself as a Senior Management Services Consultant for a public accounting firm. In 10 years, my goal is to become a Partner for the firm.

Q. How would you describe your ideal work environment?

A. A sharing work environment. Freedom to work alone with the opportunity to be a team player and brainstorm ideas with others.

Creativity

Q. What do you do in your spare time?

A. I'm a 7-year volunteer for the Rotary Club. I like to play tennis, golf, exercise, spend quality time with my family.

Q. What was the last book you read and why did you like/dislike it?

A. *Lions Don't Need to Roar*, by Debra Benton. I thought it was quite good. It taught me how to further develop leadership power of professional presence to stand out, fit in, and move ahead on the job.

Compatibility

Q. What interests you about our organization?

A. Your reputation of valuing your employees and of giving them the opportunity to perform to and above their potential. Your state-of-the-art equipment.

Q. How would your co-workers rate you as a team player?

A. I work very well as a team member.

Q. Why are you leaving your current company?

A. My (wife/husband) received a promotion and we are needing to relocate. (Or) I am looking for a firm that offers more educational opportunity and room for advancement within the company.

Q. What do you expect to get from this position that you're not getting now?

A. Job satisfaction, personal growth, and a better benefit package for my family.

SAMPLE QUESTIONNAIRE FOR A CHIEF EXECUTIVE OFFICER (CEO) POSITION

The following questions are from a questionnaire used by a head-hunting firm to locate a Chief Executive Officer (CEO) for one of its corporate clients. My client and I brainstormed together to come up with these answers:

Q. Outline as best you can, what your priorities/goals would be for the first six months with the corporation?

A. I would set out immediately to reverse the downward trend in unit sales and price per unit experienced in the first quarter of 1992. To do this, I would become familiar with the company including the physical plant, its systems, procedures, and financial conditions. I would evaluate the operation of the company and its personnel. I would then institute changes as necessary to improve the company's performance and morale.

Q. What results will you personally look for to determine if you are making a contribution to the corporation at the end of the first year?

A. At the end of the first year, I plan to have a smooth working team to further the profitable growth of the company. I expect the second year to show a marked improvement in productivity and profits.

Q. Describe in some detail the communication styles/process/tools you use to support and encourage employees in an organization of this size?

A. Communication is one of the most important and complex elements of a successful organization. First, I need to know the type of information to be transmitted, where it is to be sent, and how many people and locations would receive the communiques before I could accurately recommend the style, process, or tools to be used.

Q. Describe your leadership style and explain why that works well for the organization?

A. I am a hands-on manager acting as an excellent role model. I delegate authority well with the natural ability to gain respect with professionals and nonprofessionals at all levels.

Q. What qualities do you look for in hiring new people and developing current employees?

A. Loyalty, leadership skills, team player, intelligence, organizational skills with a positive attitude, and the ability and motivation to follow a job or task through to completion while maintaining strict deadline schedules.

Q. What would former employers describe as a sampling of your personal qualities?

A. That I am loyal, dedicated, team leader/player, well organized, knowledgeable, innovative and detail oriented, and have effective managerial skills in all aspects of business.

Q. What do you think former employees would say about working for you?

A. That I am fair, firm, loyal, demanding, and honest.

Q. Have you provided all that is needed to market your candidacy against the competition?

A. My present position represents three separate areas of responsibility. First, the duties of Chief Executive Officer. Second, for our parent company, I manage the warehousing facilities. Third, I am general manager of one division that owns and operates four franchises located throughout the western states. I am very good at what I do and am proud of the successes I have achieved.

QUESTIONS FOR YOU TO ASK THE INTERVIEWER

1. What's your turnover rate for (your own profession)?

2. What's your usage rate of temporary staff?

3. What kind of advancement opportunities do you have to offer?

4. Does the firm (or other company or corporation) provide in-services and continued educational opportunities or do I have to go outside? For example: Do they offer certification in speciality areas?

5. Before you are offered a position, always ask if you can speak to staff members about the job.

6. Do you offer incentive programs? For instance, do you offer a relocation package if you are hired from out-of-state? (I know of companies that do not offer incentive programs but do offer great educational opportunities and provide in-services, excellent benefit packages, advancement opportunities, and certification programs. Their turnover rate is less than 1 percent.)

REMEMBER: JOB SATISFACTION, BENEFIT PACKAGE, PHILOSOPHY, AND VALUING EMPLOYEES CAN BE WORTH A LOT MORE THAN AN INCENTIVE PROGRAM.

REFERENCES AND LETTERS OF RECOMMENDATION

Most employers will ask for three personal and/or business references. The list of persons who will give you a reference should include names, professional titles, organizations they work for, and organization addresses and phone numbers. Always let your contacts know that you plan to use their name as a reference and make sure they will give you a *good* one. It's usually unnecessary to mail references with your resume and cover letter unless requested. It is, however, a good idea to bring them with you to the interview along with a letter of recommendation. A letter of recommendation is the letter written by a previous employer on the company stationery, highly recommending you for the position. If it doesn't, don't use it.

WHAT TO WEAR ON THE INTERVIEW

Always dress up for an interview. Your appearance will be the interviewer's first impression of you. Women should wear a suit, a nice dress, or skirt, blouse, and blazer. Men should wear a suit and tie; even if you know the organization's employees dress casually on the job, you are not an employee, yet. You want to look businesslike and professional. Dressing up for the interview shows the employer you take your work seriously. Believe me, it will make a difference.

10

Accountants' Associations and Publications

Accreditation Council for Accountancy and Taxation (ACAT)
1010 North Fairfax Street
Alexandria, VA 22314-1574
(703) 549-6400

Nonmembership

Publications: *Accreditation Council for Accountancy and Taxation—Action Letter; Accreditation Council for Accountancy and Taxation Directory*

ACPA International (ACPA)
11 Harristown Road
Glen Rock, NJ 07452
(201) 444-7756

Members: 55

Publications: *ACPA Directory; ACPA International Quarterly Newsletter; ACPA International Reference Manual; ACPA Brochure*

American Accounting Association (AAA)
5717 Bessie Drive
Sarasota, FL 34233-2399
(813) 921-7747

Members: 12,000

Publications: *Accounting Horizons; Accounting Review; Issues in Accounting Education; Newsletter*

American Association of Attorney-Certified Public Accountants (AAA-CPA)
24196 Alicia Parkway, Suite K
Mission Viejo, CA 92691
(714) 768-0336

Members: 1,350

Publications: *American Association of Attorney-Certified Public Accountants-Membership List; The Attorney-CPA; Attorney-CPA Directory*

American Association of Hispanic CPAs (AAHCPA)
1414 Metropolitan Avenue
Bronx, NY 10462
(212) 823-6144

Members: 400

Publications: *La Cuenta; Membership Directory*

American Group of CPA Firms (TAG)
1910 South Highland Avenue, Suite 210
Lombard, IL 60148
(708) 916-0300

Members: 20

Publications: *American Group Chronicle; American Group Directory of Specialized Knowledge; Client Tax Newsletter; Health Care Expertise Directory; Member Firm Confidential Statistics Report; Product Manual; Tax Expertise Directory*

American Institute of Certified Public Accountants (AICPA)
1211 Avenue of the Americas
New York, NY 10036
(212) 575-6200

Members: 280,000

Publications: *Accountants' Index, Accountants' Index Supplement; Accountants' Index Quarterly Service; Accounting Firms and Practitioners; Accounting Trends and Techniques; AICPA Washington Report; American Institute of Certified Public Accountants—Publications; CPA Client Bulletin; CPA Examinations; CPA Letter; Journal of Accountancy; Practicing CPA; Tax Adviser: A Magazine of Tax Planning, Trends and Techniques*

American Society of Tax Professionals (ASTP)
P.O. Box 1024
Sioux Falls, SD 57101
(605) 335-1185

Members: 1,000

Publication: *Tax Professional's Update*

American Society of Women Accountants (ASWA)
1755 Lynnfield Road, Suite 222
Memphis, TN 38119-7235
(901) 680-0470

Members: 8,000

Publications: *Coordinator; Membership Directory*

American Woman's Society of Certified Public Accountants
(AWSCPA)
401 North Michigan Avenue
Chicago, IL 60611
(312) 644-6610

Members: 4,000

Publications: *AWSCPA Newsletter; Issues Paper; Membership Roster*

Asian American Certified Public Accountants (AACPA)
580 California Street, 16th Floor
San Francisco, CA 94104
(415) 421-6805

Members: 200

Publications: *Asian American Certified Public Accountants—Newsletter; Director of Accounting Firms; Membership Directory*

Associated Accounting Firms International (AAFI)
1612 K Street NW, Suite 900
Washington, DC 20006
(202) 463-7900

Members: 35

Publications: *AAFI Membership Directory; Associated Accounting Firms International—Newsletter*

Associated Regional Accounting Firms (ARAF)
5950 Live Oak Parkway, No. 335
Norcross, GA 30093-1729
(404) 416-1027

Members: 58

Publications: *Marketing Services Update; Membership Directory; Quarterly Report; Resource Directory; Technical Services Update*

Association of Accounting Administrators (AAA)
7910 Woodmont Avenue, Suite 1208
Bethesda, MD 20814
(301) 913-0030

Members: 465

Publications: *AAA Membership Directory; AAA Report*

Association of Insolvency Accountants (AIA)
31332 Via Colinas, Suite 112
Westlake Village, CA 91362
(818) 889-8317

Members: 400

Publications: *Association of Insolvency Accountants Directory; Association of Insolvency Accountants Newsletter*

Association of Water Transportation Accounting Officers (AWTAO)
P.O. Box 53
Bowling Green Station
New York, NY 10004
(212) 264-1384

Members: 400

Publications: *Annual Report; Bulletin; Membership Directory*

BKR International (BKR)
233 Broadway
New York, NY 10279
(212) 766-4260

Members: 54

Publications: *Newsletter; Roster*

Continental Association of CPA Firms (CACPAF)
8301 E. Prentice Avenue, Suite 406
Englewood, CO 80111
(303) 771-4600

Members: 33

Publications: *Advantage for Health Care Providers; Banker's Advantage; Client Newsletter; Contractor's Advantage; Lawyer's Advantage; Member Newsletter; Marketing Encyclopedia*

Controllers Council (CC)
10 Paragon Drive
Montvale, NJ 07645-1760
(201) 573-6219

Members: 3,000

Publication: *Controllers Update*

Council of Petroleum Accountants Societies (COPAS)
P.O. Box 12131
Dallas, TX 75225
(214) 363-6256

Members: 3,700

Publication: *COPAS Accounts*

CPA Associates (CPAA)
230 Park Avenue, Suite 1545
New York, NY 10169
(212) 818-9700

Members: 50

Publications: *Business Advisory Client Newsletter; Construction Client Newsletter; CPA Associates Directory; Law Firm Client Newsletter; Medical Client Newsletter; Outlook; Tax Outlook; Year-End Tax Planning Guide*

Financial Accounting Foundation (FAF)
401 Merritt Seven
P.O. Box 5116
Norwalk, CT 06856
(203) 847-0700

Members: Unknown

Publications: *Financial Accounting Series; Governmental Accounting Series*

Foundation for Accounting Education (FAE)
200 Park Avenue, 10th Floor
New York, NY 10166
(212) 973-8300

Members: Unknown

Publications: *Catalog of Education Programs; Update*

Independent Accountants International (IAI)
9200 South Dadeland Boulevard, Suite 510
Miami, FL 33156
(305) 661-3580

Members: 100

Publications: *Independent Accountants International Membership Directory; Independent Accountants International Update*

Institute of Certified Management Accountants (ICMA)
10 Paragon Drive
Montgale, NJ 07645
(201) 573-6300

Members: 20,000

Publications: *CMA Roster; Newsletter*

Institute of Internal Auditors (IIA)
249 Maitland Avenue
Altamonte Springs, FL 32701-4201
(407) 830-7600

Members: 43,000

Publications: *IIA Educator; IIA Today; Institute of Internal Auditors— Membership Directory; Internal Auditor; Pistas de Auditoria; Research Reports*

Institute of Management Accountants (IMA)
10 Paragon Drive
Montvale, NJ 07645-1760
(201) 573-9000

Members: 94,000

Publications: *Association Leader; Management Accounting*

Interamerican Accounting Association (IAA)
275 Fontainebleau Boulevard
Miami, FL 33172
(305) 225-1991

Members: 28

Publications: *IAA Directory; Interamerican Accounting Magazine; Interamerican Bulletin*

International Association of Hospitality Accountants (IAHA)
P.O. Box 27649
Austin, TX 78755-2649
(512) 346-5680

Members: 3,300

Publications: *The Bottomline; International Association of Hospitality Accountants—Roster; President's Log*

International Federation of Accountants (IFAC)
540 Madison Avenue, 21st Floor
New York, NY 10022
(212) 486-2446

Members: 104

Publications: *Guidelines on Auditing, Education, Ethics, and Management Accounting; International Federation of Accountants—Annual Report; International Federation of Accountants—Newsletter*

National Association of Black Accountants (NABA)
220 I Street NE, Suite 150
Washington, DC 20002
(202) 546-6222

Members: 3,000

Publications: *Chapter to Chapter; Spectrum; Accounting—Career for All the Seasons of Your Life* (video)

National Conference of CPA Practitioners (NCCPAP)
330 West 58th Street, Suite 4C
New York, NY 10019
(212) 765-5255

Members: 1,200

Publication: *NCCPAP Newsletter*

National Office Systems Association (NOSA)
P.O. Box 8187
Silver Spring, MD 20907
(301) 589-8125

Members: 90

Publication: *NOSA Newsletter*

National Society of Accountants for Cooperatives (NSAC)
Springfield Tower Office Building
6320 Augusta Drive, Suite 800
Springfield, VA 22150
(703) 569-3088

Members: 2,050

Publications: *The Cooperative Accountant; Membership Directory*

National Society of Certified Public Accountants (NSCPA)
1313 East Sibley, Suite 201
Dolton, IL 60419
(312) 849-0098

Members: 200

Publications: None

National Society of Public Accountants (NSPA)
1010 North Fairfax Street
Alexandria, VA 22314
(703) 549-6400

Members: 23,000

Publications: *Income and Fees of Accountants in Public Practice; National Public Accountant; National Society of Public Accountants—Annual Report; National Society of Public Accountants—Yearbook; NSPA Washington Reporter*

Society of Insurance Accountants
P.O. Box 61
Hollowville, NY 12530
(518) 851-9780

Members: 900

Publication: *Society of Insurance Accountants—Roster*

Cost Management Group (CMG)
c/o Institute of Certified Management Accountants
10 Paragon Drive
Montvale, NJ 07645-1760
(201) 573-6216

Members: Unknown

Publication: *Cost Management Update*

Association of Government Accountants (AGA)
2200 Mt. Vernon Avenue
Alexandria, VA 22301
(703) 684-6931

Members: 13,000

Publications: *The Government Accountants' Journal; Government Financial Management Topics*

Governmental Accounting Standards Board (GASB)
401 Merritt Seven
P.O. Box 5116
Norwalk, CT 06856-5116
(203) 847-0700

Members: Unknown

Publication: *Governmental Accounting Standards Board—Action Report*

National Association of State Boards of Accountancy (NASBA)
545 Fifth Avenue
New York, NY 10017-3698
(212) 490-3868

Members: 54

Publications: *CPA Candidate Performance on the Uniform CPA Examination; Report of the CPA Examination Review Board; State Board Report; State Boards of Accountancy of the United States; Digest of State Accountancy Laws and State Board Regulations; Handbook and Checklist for CPA Examination Administration; Standards and Checklist for State Regulation of Public Accountancy; Model Public Accountancy Bill; Model Positive Enforcement Program*

Association for Governmental Leasing and Finance (AGLF)
1101 Connecticut Avenue, NW, Suite 700
Washington, DC 20036
(202) 429-5135

Members: 240

Publications: *Tell; Tell Flash; Governmental Leasing; Surveys of Federal Tax Law, Federal Securities Law and of Legislation and Case Law in the Fifty States*

Governmental Finance Officers Association of the United States and Canada (GFOA)
180 North Michigan Avenue, Suite 800
Chicago, IL 60601
(312) 977-9700

Members: Unknown

Publications: *Bulletin; GAAFR Review; Government Finance Officers Association—Newsletter; Government Finance Review; Public Investor*

Municipal Treasurers Association of the United States and Canada (MTA US&C)
1420 16th Street NW, Suite 401
Washington, DC 20036
(202) 797-7347

Members: 1,700

Publications: *Membership Directory; Technical Topics; Treasury Notes*

National Association of County Treasurers and Finance Officers (NACTFO)
c/o National Association of Counties
440 First Street NW, 8th Floor
Washington, DC 20001
(202) 393-6226

Members: 1,800

Publications: Unknown

National Association of State Auditors, Comptrollers, and Treasurers (NASACT)
2401 Regency Road
Lexington, KY 40503
(606) 276-1147

Members: 190

Publications: *Directory; Newsletter*

National Association of State Budget Officers (NASBO)
Hall of States
400 North Capitol Street, NW, No. 299
Washington, DC 20001
(202) 624-5382

Members: 162

Publication: *Fiscal Survey of the States*

National Association of State Treasurers (NAST)
c/o Council of State Governments
Iron Works Pike
P.O. Box 11910
Lexington, KY 40578
(606) 252-2291

Members: 75

Publications: *Directory; Newsletter; State Treasury Profiles*

Society of Financial Examiners (SOFE)
4101 Lake Boone Trail, Suite 201
Raleigh, NC 27607
(800) 962-2384

Members: 2,100

Publications: *AGB Notes; AGB Reports*

Association of School Business Officials International (ASBO)
11401 North Shore Drive
Reston, VA 22090
(703) 478-0405

Members: 6,900

Publications: *ASBO Accents; School Business Affairs*

American Taxation Association (ATA)
c/o American Accounting Association
5717 Bessie Drive
Sarasota, FL 34233
(813) 921-7747

Members: 1,250

Publications: *Journal of the American Taxation Association; Newsletter*

Center for Local Tax Research (CITR)
121 East 30th Street
New York, NY 10016
(212) 889-8020

Members: Unknown

Publication: *Incentive Taxation*

Coalition Against Regressive Taxation (CART)
c/o Ken Stinger
430 First Street SE
Washington, DC 20003
(202) 544-6245

Members: Unknown

Federation of Tax Administrators (FTA)
444 North Capitol Street, Suite 334
Washington, DC 20001
(202) 624-5890

Members: Unknown

Publications: *State Legal Issues Quarterly; Tax Administrators News*

Institute for Certification of Tax Professionals (ICTP)
1832 Stratford Place
Pomona, CA 91768
(714) 629-1460

Members: Unknown

Publication: *The Tax Professional*

Institute of Property Taxation (IPT)
888 17th Street, NW, Suite 1150
Washington, DC 20006
(202) 452-1213

Members: 2,800

Publications: *Institute of Property Taxation—Membership Directory; Property Tax Report; Sales Tax Report; Property Taxation*

Institute of Tax Consultants (ITC)
7500 212th SW, No. 205
Edmonds, WA 98026
(206) 774-3521

Members: Unknown

Publications: None

International Association of Assessing Officers (IAAO)
1313 East 60th Street
Chicago, IL 60637-2892
(312) 947-2069

Members: 8,300

Publications: *Assessment Digest; Assessment and Valuation Legal Reporter; CAAS News; International Association of Assessing Officers—Bibliographic Series; International Association of Assessing Officers—Membership Directory; International Association of Assessing Officers—Research and Information Series; Mapping Section News; Personal Property Section News; Property Tax Journal*

International Tax Institute (ITI)
c/o Alan O. Dixler
Merck & Co., Inc.
P.O. Box 2000
Rahway, NJ 07065
(908) 594-7295

Members: Unknown

Publications: *International Tax Institute—Report to Members; Seminar Proceedings Manual; Volumes of Speakers*

Multistate Tax Commission (MTC)
444 North Capitol Street, NW, Suite 409
Washington, DC 20001
(202) 624-8699

Members: 30

Publication: *Corporate Tax Handbook*

National Association of Computerized Tax Processors (NACTP)
c/o Mr. L.D. Caracciolo
2670 Cunningham Hole Road
Annapolis, MD 21401
(301) 266-8560

Members: 75

Publication: *NACTP Directory*

National Association of Enrolled Agents (NAEA)
6000 Executive Boulevard, Suite 205
Rockville, MD 20852
(301) 984-6232

Members: 7,000

Publications: *EA; EAlert; NAEA Annual Membership Directory*

National Association of Enrolled Federal Tax Accountants (NAEFTA)
6108 North Harding Avenue
Chicago, IL 60659-3108
(312) 463-5577

Members: Unknown

Publication: *The EFTA*

National Association of Tax Consultors (NATC)
454 North 13th Street
San Jose, CA 95112
(408) 298-1458

Members: 2,000

Publication: *National Consultor*

National Association of Tax Practitioners (NATP)
720 Association Drive
Appleton, WI 54914
(414) 749-1040

Members: 13,400

Publications: *Buyer's Guide; NATP Report; Tax Software Survey; 1040 Report; Who's Who in Tax Preparation*

National Tax Association—Tax Institute of America (NTA-TIA)
5310 East Main Street, Suite 104
Columbus, OH 43213
(614) 864-1221

Members: 1,800

Publications: *National Tax Association—Tax Institute of America—Proceedings of the Annual Conference; National Tax Journal*

National Tax Equality Association (NTEA)
1629 K Street, NW, Suite 1000
Washington, DC 20006
(202) 466-8308

Members: 400

Publication: *Washington Report*

Research Institute of America (RIA)
90 5th Avenue
New York, NY 10011
(212) 645-4800

Nonmembership

Publication: Catalog

Tax Council (TC)
1801 K Street NW, No. 7204
Washington, DC 20006
(202) 822-8062

Members: 95

Publications: *Program Policy Booklet; Tax Legislative Bulletin; Working Papers*

Tax Executives Institute (TEI)
1001 Pennsylvania Avenue, NW, Suite 320
Washington, DC 20004-2505
(202) 638-5601

Members: 4,700

Publication: *The Tax Executive*

Tax Foundation (TF)
470 L'Enfant Plaza East SW, Suite 7400
Washington, DC 20024
(202) 863-5454

Members: 2,800

Publications: *Facts and Figures on Government Finance; Issue Briefs; Proceedings; Special Reports; Tax Features*

Beta Alpha Psi
5717 Bessie Drive
Sarasota, FL 34233
(813) 924-7818

Members: 170,000

Publications: *Chapter Directories; Newsletter*

Accountants for the Public Interest
1012 14th Street, NW, Suite 906
Washington, DC 20005
(202) 347-1668

Members: 2,000

Publications: *API Account; National Directory of Volunteer Accounting Programs; What a Difference Nonprofits Make: A Guide to Accounting Procedures*

Association of Healthcare Internal Auditors (AHIA)
5700 Old Orchard Road, 1st Floor
Skokie, IL 60077-1024
(708) 966-6636

Members: 900

Publications: *Membership Directory; New Perspectives*

Healthcare Financial Management Association (HFMA)
Two Westbrook Corporate Center, Suite 700
Westchester, IL 60154
(708) 531-9600

Members: 27,000

Publications: *Healthcare Financial Management; Notes from National; Patient Accounts*

Institute of Certified Professional Business Consultants (ICPBC) (Medical Administration)
600 South Federal Street, Suite 400
Chicago, IL 60605
(312) 922-6222

Members: 270

Publications: *Institute of Certified Professional Business Consultants—Membership Directory; Institute of Certified Professional Business Consultants—Newsletter*

Academy of Accounting Historians (AAH)
James Madison University
School of Accounting
Harrisonburg, VA 22807
(703) 568-3084

Members: 850

Publications: *Accounting Historians Journal; Accounting Historians Notebook; Membership Directory; Monograph Series*

Data Processing Management Association (DPMA)
505 Busse Highway
Park Ridge, IL 60068
(708) 825-8124

Members: 40,000

Publications: *Information Executive; Inside DAMA*

Accountants Computer Users Technical Exchange (ACUTE)
6081 East 82nd Street, Suite 110
Indianapolis, IN 46250
(317) 845-8702

Members: 385

Publications: *The Account; Accountants Computer Users Technical Exchange—Membership Directory*

National Accounting and Finance Council (NAFC) (Transportation Industry)
2200 Mill Road
Alexandria, VA 22314
(703) 838-1915

Members: 1,100

Publications: *ATA Accounting Service; Bulletin; Motor Carrier Credit and Collection Practices Manual; Motor Freight Controller; NAFC Federal Excise Tax Guide; NAFC Membership Directory; NAFC Risk Management Manual for Motor Carriers; NAFC Sales Tax Service; NAFC State Tax Guide; NAFC Tax Information Service; Workers' Compensation Newsletter*

Association of American Railroads (AAR) (Economics and Finance)
Library Room 5800
50 F Street, NW
Washington, DC 20001
(202) 639-2333

Members: 110

Publications: *Official Railway Equipment Register; Rail News Update; Railroad Facts*

Insurance Accounting and Systems Association (IASA)
P.O. Box 51340
Durham, NC 27717
(919) 489-0991

Members: 1,700

Publications: *The Interpreter; Proceedings; Life Accounting Textbook; Property and Liability Accounting Textbook*

Associated Minicomputer Dealers of America (AMDA)
3101 North Central Avenue, Suite 560
Phoenix, AZ 85012
(602) 265-1699

Members: 71

Formerly: Accounting Machine Dealers Association of America (1977); Accounting Machine Minicomputer Dealers of America (1983)

Publications: *Associated Minicomputer Dealers of America—Newsletter; Associated Minicomputer Dealers of America—Yearbook*

11

Resume Samples for Accountants and Financial Professionals

The following pages include many resume samples from the accounting and finance client files of Just Resumes. Others were prepared specifically for this book. All these samples offer accurate job descriptions and educational requirement information. The educational requirements vary from state to state, and the job titles and descriptions vary from each government, public, or private accounting corporation or organization.

The following resume samples cover professionals from public, government, and private sectors; each resume focuses on particular individual goals. There are a variety of formats to choose from in functional, chronological, and combination styles. An index to the resume samples appears at the back of the book. The resumes are listed in alphabetical order and are conveniently categorized by job title.

Look at each resume carefully. Think about how your own background applies to the job or internship you'd like to obtain.

Remember, it's important for you to have already read Chapters 1 and 2 before reviewing the samples in this chapter. With this approach, you can take full advantage of the valuable information in this book by gaining the overall perspective you'll need to write your own effective resume.

ETHAN LAWRENCE MANNING
2390 West Elizabeth Street
Ft. Collins, CO 80521
(303) 223-2209

OBJECTIVE
A Senior Accountant position

PROFESSIONAL EXPERIENCE

ACCOUNTANT I   1988-91
State of Alabama, State Controller's Office
- Prepare vouchers and journal entries to effect adjustments, transfers and corrections to the general ledger and the Agency Budget Ledger of central accounting authorities.
- Review fiscal source documents for completeness, mathematical accuracy, paper authorization, sufficiency of information, proper coding, and proper application of fees, refunds, collections, taxes, and discounts.
- Notify other related agency personnel of incorrectly filled out accounting documentation and request revised paperwork.
- Reconcile discrepancies by resolving flagged error listing on computer runs, cross checking source documentation, or balancing figures.
- Examine fiscal and accounting records to determine the sufficiency of funds or to establish spending limitation figures.
- Reconcile two sets of accounting records to each other to achieve a proper balance.
- Accumulate and consolidate data for fiscal reports for review by higher professional accounting and administrative personnel.
- Review transactions to assure conformance to statutes, rules, regulations, and procedures governing such items.
- Post items to specific assigned journals and ledgers.
- Adjust, close, and balance accounts and prepare year-end statements under the supervision or direction of a higher level professional accountant.

EDUCATION
BBA, Public Administration, 1988
University of Alabama at Birmingham

PROFESSIONAL PROFILE
- Considerable knowledge of general accounting principles.
- Knowledge of governmental accounting, internal and external auditing, budgeting and direct and indirect costing methods.
- Knowledgeable in depreciation accounting, inventory control and debt financing.
- Excellent written and verbal communication skills.

PREVIOUS EMPLOYMENT HISTORY
Accounting Clerk Intern, State of Alabama, Controller's Office   1984-88
Accounting Clerk, University of Alabama at Birmingham   Summers 1980-84

IRVING S. WEISSMAN
320 East Elizabeth Street
Ft. Collins, CO 80524
(303) 224-4509

OBJECTIVE
A Senior Accountant position

PROFESSIONAL EXPERIENCE
ACCOUNTANT II   1991-present
State of Colorado, State Controller's Office
* Analyze funds and fund structures to determine problems, suggest corrections, and make modifications.
* Review financial problems and analyze statutes to assure that transactions meet statutory requirements.
* Analyze chart of accounts and make appropriate additions and deletions.
* Prepare substantive financial statements.
* Analyze accounting systems and identify proper accounting controls. Suggest or install new controls or modify current controls.
* Devise systems of programs requiring the application of cost accounting and indirect and direct costing procedures.
* Establish methods and systems in inventory control, accounts receivable, cash disbursements, depreciation accounting, and debt financing.
* Analyze expenditure controls and assure that funds are expended for authorized purposes only and within previously determined limits.
* Make budgetary and accounting decisions when expenditure controls are or are about to be exceeded.
* Train and supervise technical and clerical accounting employees.

EDUCATION
BBA, Public Administration, 1988
University of Denver, Denver, CO

PROFESSIONAL PROFILE
* Thorough knowledge of general accounting principles.
* Considerable knowledge of governmental accounting, internal and external auditing, budgeting and direct and indirect costing methods.
* Knowledgeable in depreciation accounting, inventory control and debt financing.
* Ability to train and supervise technical and clerical staff while maintaining effective working relationships with others.
* Excellent written and verbal communication skills.

PREVIOUS EMPLOYMENT HISTORY
Accountant 1, State of Alabama, Controller's Office   1988-91
Accounting Clerk, University of Denver, Denver, CO   Summers 1984-88

REBA S. WASHINGTON
2315 Kittery Court
Ft. Collins, CO 80525
(303) 226-0034

OBJECTIVE
A Senior Accountant Position

PROFESSIONAL EXPERIENCE

ACCOUNTANT III   1982-present
State of Colorado, State Controller's Office
- Supervise professional and technical accounting personnel.
- Calculate end of fiscal year accounting adjustments.
- Insure that the operation of the accounting system is carried out in compliance with applicable rules, laws, policies and procedures.
- Determine whether the fullest disclosure of financial operations is provided by system.
- Modify accounting systems by noting problems, revising procedures, and recommending and/or implementing new methods.
- Develop and initiate sophisticated accounting controls to prove the validity of data.
- Authorize and develop modifications in the coding structure of accounting system.
- Develop and implement additional accounting reports, new and revised cost accounting systems and procedures.

EDUCATION
MBA, Accounting, 1982
University of Alabama at Birmingham

BBA, Public Administration, 1975
University of Texas at Austin

PROFESSIONAL PROFILE
- Gained thorough knowledge of governmental accounting, budgeting, and internal and external auditing.
- Familiar with cost accounting including direct and indirect costing methods.
- Familiar with specialized accounting such as depreciation accounting, inventory control and debt financing.
- Prepare comprehensive financial statements, special reports, systems analysis, sub-systems, and operating sub-systems with little or no supervision.
- Developed excellent verbal and written communication skills.
- Train and supervise others with diplomacy and tact, demonstrating effective team player and leadership skills.

PREVIOUS EMPLOYMENT HISTORY
Accountant II, State of Alabama, Controller's Office   1979-82
Accountant I, State of Texas's Controller's Office   1975-79

JULIE ANNE WERSOLOTTE
980 Wichita Avenue
Ft. Collins, CO 80525
(303) 226-3029

OBJECTIVE
An Accountant/Manager position

PROFESSIONAL EXPERIENCE
ACCOUNTANT IV   1990-present
State of Colorado, State Controller's Office
- Calculate end of fiscal year accounting adjustments.
- Interpret and explain the state controller's fiscal rules or policies and the meaning of various accounting theory to accounting staff.
- Insure that the operation of accounting systems are carried out in compliance with government rules, laws, policies and procedures.
- Interpret rules, regulations and laws in arriving at decisions of how accounting transactions or systems should be handled.
- Determine whether the fullest disclosure of financial operations is provided by the accounting system.
- Modify accounting systems by noting problems, revising procedures and recommending and implementing new methods.
- Initiate use of sophisticated accounting controls to prove the validity of data or system.
- Develop, implement and authorize use of modifications in the coding structure of the accounting system as well as additional accounting reports.
- Create and implement the use of new and revised cost accounting system and procedures.
- Supervise professional and technical accounting personnel.

PROFESSIONAL PROFILE
- Developed comprehensive knowledge of general, cost and governmental accounting.
- Thorough knowledge in depreciation accounting, inventory control, and debt financing.
- Ability to prepare comprehensive financial statements and special reports.
- Perform management, systems analysis of accounting systems and sub-systems.
- Communicate effectively orally and in writing, especially concerning professional accounting procedures, practices and methods.
- Demonstrate excellent team player/leadership skills.

EDUCATION
BBA, Accounting, 1978
University of Texas at Austin

PREVIOUS EMPLOYMENT HISTORY
Accountant III, State of Colorado, State Controller's Office   1985-90
Accountant II, State of Louisiana, State Controller's Office   1981-85
Accountant I, State of Louisiana, State Controller's Office   1978-81

JESSE J. GUZMAN
2398 Kittery Court
Ft. Collins, CO 80525
(303) 226-0039

OBJECTIVE
An Accountant position with a Property Management Corporation

PROFESSIONAL EXPERIENCE
ACCOUNTANT
The Group, Incorporated, Ft. Collins, CO   1985-present
- Identify and keep records of company owned or leased equipment, buildings, and other property.

- Record description, value, location, and other information of each item.

- Conduct periodic inventories to keep records current and ensure that equipment is properly maintained.

- Distribute cost of maintenance to proper accounts.

- Examine records to determine that acquisition, sale, retirement, and other entries have been made.

- Prepare statements reflecting monthly appreciated and depreciated values.

- Summarize statement on annual basis for income tax purposes.

- Prepare schedules for amortization of buildings and equipment.

- Develop and recommend property accounting methods to provide effective controls.

EDUCATION
MBA, Accounting, 1978
California State University, at Los Angeles

BA, Accounting, 1974
University of Denver, Denver, CO

PREVIOUS EMPLOYMENT HISTORY
Accountant, Property Management Incorporated, Los Angeles, CA   1978-85
Accountant, Glenhaven Property Management, Denver, CO   1974-78

PAUL C. CARLSON, C.P.A.
213 City Park Drive
Ft. Collins, CO 80524
(303) 224-5432

OBJECTIVE
A Cost Accountant position

PROFESSIONAL EXPERIENCE

Financial Accounting
- Prepared financial statements under cash and accrual accounting methods for sole proprietorships, partnerships, S and nonprofit corporations.
- Processed automated payroll and filed quarterly tax reports.
- Administrated defined contribution, profit sharing and cafeteria plans.
- Held responsible for capital purchases, leasing contacts, and maintenance agreements for plant assets.
- Maintained accounts receivable for private water companies and homeowner's assn.
- Solved collection problems in a diplomatic and courteous manner, under sometimes sensitive situations.

Cost Accounting
- Assisted product line controller in preparation of labor variance reports and departmental forecasts.
- Generated report for annual audit.

Computer Experience
- Designed custom spreadsheet programs for internal use and for clients.
- Converted manual accounting systems to computerized general ledger, accounts receivable, accounts payable, and payroll systems.

Management and Administration
- Trained and supervised accounts receivable, payroll, and purchasing staff.
- Maintained group health insurance, workman's compensation, general liability and automobile insurance policies.

PROFESSIONAL AFFILIATIONS
Member, American Accounting Association
Member, American Institute of Certified Public Accountants

EDUCATION
BA, Accounting, 1985
University of Denver, Denver, CO

PREVIOUS EMPLOYMENT HISTORY

Staff Accountant, Sherwood Corporation, Denver, CO	1988-present
Staff Accountant, Public Accounting Firm, Denver, CO	1985-88

MICHAEL FOREST SHANNON
1245 Terry Shores Drive
Ft. Collins, CO 80524
(303) 224-9543

OBJECTIVE
A Controller position

PROFESSIONAL EXPERIENCE

ASSISTANT CONTROLLER   1985-present
Atlantic Piston Rings, Denver, CO

- Provided directors with more accurate reports and forecasts based on realistic feedbacks from dealers and salesmen.

- Reduced inventory levels by coordinating purchasing and production with sales backlog and forecasts.

- Assisted departmental heads to work within strict budgets and cut costs.

- Improved relations with bankers and obtained their approval on a deferred payment plan on the company's delinquent loan.

- Prepared corporate and franchise tax forms, budgets, forecasts, cash flow analysis and quotes for large orders or unusual configurations.

- Reviewed letters of credit.

- Reduced accounting department's work load by simplifying flow of documents, eliminating unnecessary reports and converting payroll schedule from weekly to biweekly.

EDUCATION
MBA, Accounting, 1978
California State University, Los Angeles

BA, Accounting, 1974
University of Denver, Denver, CO

PREVIOUS EMPLOYMENT HISTORY

Cost Accountant Manager, Atlantic Piston Rings, Los Angeles, CA   1978-85
Cost Accountant, Wyatt Corporation, Denver, CO   1974-78

STEPHEN S. BROCK
9876 Rustic Road
Santa Barbara, CA 93110
(805) 569-1234

Objective: An Assistant Treasurer position

PROFESSIONAL EXPERIENCE

Treasury Operations
- Monitored the accounting of short-term investment portfolios:
  - Clarified corporate objectives and long term goals;
  - Assessed financial resources and tolerance for risk.
- Prepared and filed SEC related reports:
  - Annual reports...10K's...shareholder reports...10Q's.
- Established pension plans for businesses nationwide.

Management & Administration
- Supervised staff to insure accuracy of the pricing, billing and inventory control systems for a Fortune 500 corporation.
- Key member in the conversion and update of a more efficient computerized inventory and distribution system.
- Established/approved credit for product and service oriented corporations.
- Trained, supervised and reviewed financial operations personnel.

Investor Relations/Communications
- Successfully fulfill investor relations function:
  - Key source of daily information for investors and financial analysts;
  - Liaison between treasury department, transfer agents and trustees.
- Delivered effective presentations on financial disclosure issues to in-house functional managers, in conjunction with upcoming press releases.

EDUCATION
BS Degree, Accounting - 1980
Pennsylvania State University

EMPLOYMENT HISTORY

Financial Accounts Manager, TMC Corporation, Santa Barbara, CA	1988-present
Treasury Operations Analyst, ABC Corporation, Los Angeles, CA	1983-88
Regional Credit Manager, Northern Inc, Long Beach, CA	1980-83

SHERRY CLAIRMONT, C.P.A.
4570 West Elizabeth
Ft. Collins, CO 80524
(303) 224-5403

OBJECTIVE
Audit Manager

PROFESSIONAL EXPERIENCE

AUDIT MANAGER   1988-present
Coopers & Lybrand, Denver, CO

- Delegate audit field work and assignment of detailed audit work to Staff.

- Review audit working papers and financial statement disclosure footnote for approval.

- Serve as public representative to the firm, maintaining day-to-day client relationships.

- Determine billings for engagements.

- Approve entire auditing program.

- Schedule auditing personnel staff.

- Supervise, train, and evaluate Senior and Staff Auditors.

PROFESSIONAL AFFILIATIONS
Member, American Accounting Association
Member, American Institute of Certified Public Accountants

EDUCATION
MBA, Accounting, 1988
California State University, Los Angeles

BA, Accounting, 1982
University of Denver, Denver, CO
C.P.A. Exam: Passed 1982

PREVIOUS EMPLOYMENT HISTORY
Senior Auditor, Coopers & Lybrand, Los Angeles, CA   1986-88
Staff Auditor, Joyce & Associates, Denver, CO   1982-86

SUSAN BARBARA FREEMAN
5954 Overland Trail
Ft. Collins, CO 80521
(303) 224-5403

OBJECTIVE
Audit Manager

PROFESSIONAL EXPERIENCE

SENIOR AUDITOR   1988-present
Deloitte & Touche, Denver, CO
- Work directly under the Audit Manager to delegate audit field work and assign detailed work to Staff Associates.

- Review working papers and consult with Audit Staff.

- Prepare financial statements.

- Develop corporate tax returns and suggest improvements to internal controls.

PROFESSIONAL AFFILIATIONS
Member, American Accounting Association
Member, American Institute of Certified Public Accountants

EDUCATION
MBA, Accounting, 1988
California State University, Los Angeles

BA, Accounting, 1985
University of Denver, Denver, CO
CPA Exam: Passed 1985

PREVIOUS EMPLOYMENT HISTORY
Senior Auditor, Ernst & Young, Los Angeles, CA   1987-88
Staff Auditor, Drake & Associates, Denver, CO   1985-87
Auditing Intern, Russell & Associates, Denver, CO   1983-85

TERRY YOKAHAMA, C.P.A.
3029 Dunbar Street
Ft. Collins, CO 80526
(303) 223-0049

OBJECTIVE
Staff Auditor

PROFESSIONAL EXPERIENCE

STAFF AUDITOR   1985-present
Charles & Associates, C.P.A., Denver, CO
- Examine and analyze accounting records for large and small businesses throughout the county to determine financial status.

- Prepare financial reports concerning operating procedures.

- Review data regarding material assets, net worth, liabilities, capital stock, surplus, income, and expenditures.

- Inspect items in books of original entry to determine if accepted accounting procedure was followed in recording transactions.

- Count cash on hand, inspect notes receivable and payable, negotiable securities, and canceled checks.

- Verify journal and ledger entries of cash and check payments, purchases, expenses, and trial balances by examining and authenticating inventory items.

- Prepare reports for management concerning scope of audit, financial conditions found, and source and application of funds.

- Recommend improvement of operations for financial position of company.

- Supervise and coordinate activities of auditors specializing in specific operations of business undergoing audit.

EDUCATION
BA, Accounting, 1974
University of Denver, Denver, CO

PREVIOUS EMPLOYMENT HISTORY
Certified Public Accountant, Drake & Associates, Denver, CO   1978-85
Staff Auditor, Prudential Insurance, Denver, CO   1974-78

NOELLA CHRISTOPHER
690 10th Street
Boulder, CO 80302
(303) 449-1123

Objective: An Auditor position

PROFESSIONAL PROFILE

- Highly organized, dedicated with a positive attitude.
- Ability to handle multiple assignments in highly pressured situations and consistently meet tight deadline schedules.
- Thorough and committed to professionalism; thrive on opportunities to assume responsibility.

PROFESSIONAL EXPERIENCE

Proposal Audit/Incurred Cost Audit
- Successfully perform audits of small and intermediate contractors throughout Santa Barbara as an active member of the mobile team.
  - Evaluate proposals to determine reasonableness, accuracy and compliance with government regulations.

Labor Floor Check
- Review contractors labor charging and allocation system to determine the adequacy of contractors' labor policies, procedures and internal controls.
  - Recommend improvements to comply with government regulations.

Accounting System Review
- Analyze contractors' accounting systems and internal controls to determine adequacy of accumulating and segregating costs for government contracts.

EDUCATION

BS Degree, Business, Accounting Emphasis
University of Colorado, Boulder, CO, 1987

AA Degree, Business Economics, 1984
Kinsborough Community College, Brooklyn, NY

EMPLOYMENT HISTORY

Home Management, Travel, Study	1991-present
Auditor, Santa Barbara Auditing Service	1987-91
Auditor, Boulder Bank & Trust, Boulder, CO	1984-87

SUSANNE M. LEW
2926 Jakonda Drive
Ft. Collins, CO 80525
(303) 224-5501

OBJECTIVE
A Data Processing Auditor Management position

PROFESSIONAL EXPERIENCE

HEWLETT PACKARD, Ft. Collins, CO   1986-present
Auditor, Information Systems

- Plan and conduct audits of data processing systems and applications to safeguard assets, ensure accuracy of data, and promote operational efficiency.

- Establish audit objectives and devise audit plan, following general audit plan and previous audit reports.

- Interview workers and examine computerized records to gather data.

- Analyze data gathered to evaluate effectiveness of controls and determine accuracy of reports and efficiency and security of operations.

- Write computerized audit report to document findings and recommendations.

- Devise, write, and test computer program required to obtain information needed for audit.

- Devise controls for new or modified computer application to prevent inaccurate calculations and data loss, and to ensure discovery of errors.

EDUCATION
MBA, Accounting, 1986
California State University, at Los Angeles

BA, Computer Science, 1974
University of Denver, Denver, CO

PREVIOUS EMPLOYMENT HISTORY
Systems Analyst, IBM Corporation, Los Angeles, CA   1978-86
Computer Programmer, Information Systems Associates, Ft. Collins, CO   1974-78

ANTHONY B. BINGHAM
9001 Constitution Avenue
Ft. Collins, CO 80526
(303) 225-0039

OBJECTIVE
A Budget Accountant position

PROFESSIONAL EXPERIENCE
BUDGET ACCOUNTANT   1981-present
Anheuser Busch, Incorporated, Ft. Collins, CO

- Develop and install computerized budgeting system for entire corporation.

- Analyze past and present financial operations and estimate future revenues and expenditures to prepare budget.

- Document revenues and expenditures expected and submit to management.

- Analyze computerized records of present and past operations, trends and costs, estimated and realized revenues, administrative commitments, and obligations incurred to project future revenues and expenses.

- Maintain budgeting system which provides control of expenditures made to carry out advertising and marketing, production, maintenance, and special project activities such as construction of buildings.

- Advise management on matters such as effective use of resources and assumptions underlying budget forecasts.

- Interpret budgets to management.

EDUCATION
MBA, Accounting, 1978
University of Hartford, CT

BA, Business Administration, 1974
University of Denver, Denver, CO

PREVIOUS EMPLOYMENT HISTORY
Senior Accountant, ABC Corporation, Denver, CO   1978-81
Staff Accountant, LB Ski Industries, Inc., Denver, CO   1974-78

HARVEY THOMAS LANDERS
212 Whitcomb Street
Ft. Collins, CO 80524
(303) 223-0384

OBJECTIVE
Budget Analyst

PROFESSIONAL EXPERIENCE
POLICY/BUDGET ANALYST

State of Colorado, Office of State Planning and Budgeting   1987-present

- Identify policy issues, their analysis and review, and the development of alternatives and recommendations.
- Review policy proposals and budget requests and recommend changes based on analysis or support budget estimate and requests.
  - Compare to other states and jurisdictions statistical analyses of program workload or output and staff utilization.
- Participate in the presentation of issues, alternatives, and recommendations to agency personnel and Department Heads, the Governor, the Joint Budget Committee, OSPB staff, and other appropriate groups in the legislature.
- Monitor the agency program and budget execution.
  - Recommendation of funding requirements within authorized limits.
  - Review and approval of financial plans and allotments.
  - Periodic review of the encumbrances and expenditure of funds, central POT transfers, and review of supplemental requests.
- Advise and assist operating managers concerning guidelines for budget formulation and execution.
  - Ways to better utilize funds and personnel, and solve management problems.
- Review and approve or disapprove, as delegated, requests for transfers of funds, funding of personnel actions, new accounts, roll-forwards, and contracts.
- Prepare the periodic program and financial management reports for the Governor and the Executive Director.

PROFESSIONAL PROFILE
- Knowledge of principles of governmental accounting and finance.
- Gained excellent management skills, including personnel management, organizational structure, and delegation of authority.

EDUCATION
Master's Degree, Public Administration, 1987
University of Denver, Denver, CO

BBA, Business Economics, 1980
University of Texas at Austin

PREVIOUS EMPLOYMENT HISTORY
Senior Financial Analyst/Manager, First National Bank, Denver, CO   1984-87
Staff Financial Analyst, Security Bank of Texas, Austin, TX   1980-84

JOSEPH S. SCHROEDER
3240 Mountain Avenue
Ft. Collins, CO 80524
(303) 224-4512

OBJECTIVE

A Budget Analyst position

PROFESSIONAL EXPERIENCE

BUDGET ANALYST   1986-present
Larimer County, Office of Finance, Ft. Collins, CO

- Analyze current and past budgets for the Larimer County government sector.

- Prepare and justify budget requests, and allocate funds according to governmental spending priorities.

- Analyze accounting records to determine financial resources required to implement program and submit recommendations for budget allocations.

- Recommend approval or disapproval of requests for funds.

- Advise staff on cost analysis and fiscal allocations.

EDUCATION

MBA, Public Administration, 1978
University of Texas at Austin

BA, Accounting, 1974
University of Denver, Denver, CO

PREVIOUS EMPLOYMENT HISTORY

Budget Analyst, City of Austin, Austin, TX   1978-86
Staff Accountant, The Borden Company, Denver, CO   1974-78

MARVIN P. MATLIN
5401 Constitution Court
Ft. Collins, CO 80525
(303) 225-0032

OBJECTIVE
A Budget Analyst position

PROFESSIONAL EXPERIENCE

BUDGET ANALYST   1989-present
Allied Products Corporation, Ft. Collins, CO
- Provide advice and technical assistance in the preparation of annual budgets working closely with the chief financial officer.
- Review proposed operating and financial plans—proposed program increases or new initiatives, estimated costs and expenses, and capital expenditures needed to finance these programs for the County of Larimer.
- Examine the budget estimates for completeness, accuracy, and conformance with procedures, regulations, and organizational objectives.
- Review financial requests by employing cost-benefit analysis, assessing program trade-offs, and exploring alternative funding methods.
- Examine past and current budgets, and research economic developments that affect the county's spending.
- Consolidate each department's budgets into operating and financial budget summaries and submit preliminary budgets to senior management with comments and supporting statements to justify or deny funding requests.
- Monitor the operating budget by reviewing periodic reports and accounting records to determine if allocated funds have been spent as specified.
- Assist in developing procedural guidelines and policies governing the development, formulation, and maintenance of the budget.
- Conduct training sessions for company personnel of new budget procedures.

EDUCATION

PhD, University of Texas at Austin, 1984

BBA, Accounting, 1978
University of Texas at Austin

PREVIOUS EMPLOYMENT HISTORY

Internal Audit Manager, Allied Products Corp., Denver, CO   1984-89
Senior Internal Auditor, Industrial Equipment Corp., Austin, TX   1980-84
Staff Internal Auditor, Industrial Equipment Corp., Austin, TX   1978-80

JESSICA CARA CASPER
3209 W. Mulberry Street
Ft. Collins, CO 80521
(303) 224-5843

OBJECTIVE
A Budget Director position

PROFESSIONAL EXPERIENCE

BUDGET OFFICER

Cerabral Palsy Foundation, Denver, CO   1984-present

- Direct and coordinate activities of personnel responsible to formulate, monitor and present budgets for controlling funds to implement program objectives.

- Correlate appropriations for specific programs for divisional programs including items for emergency funds.

- Direct compilation of data based on statistical studies and analyses of past and current years to prepare budgets and to justify funds requested.

- Review operating budgets to analyze trends affecting budget needs.

- Consult with unit heads to ensure adjustments are made in accordance with program changes in order to facilitate long-term planning.

- Direct preparation of regular and special budget reports to interpret budget directives and to establish policies for carrying them out.

- Analyze costs in relation to services performed during previous fiscal years and submit reports to director with recommendations for budget revisions.

- Testify regarding proposed budgets before examining and fund-granting authorities to clarify reports and gain support for estimated budget needs.

- Administer personnel functions of budget department including training, work scheduling, promotions, transfers, and performance ratings.

EDUCATION
MBA, Business Administration, 1978
University of Hartford, CT

BA, Accounting, 1974
University of Denver, Denver, CO

PREVIOUS EMPLOYMENT HISTORY
Senior Budget Analyst, United Way of Hartford, Hartford, CT   1978-84
Budget Analyst/Accountant, United Way of Denver, Denver, CO   1974-78

HARRY H. KENT
2021 Southwood Drive
Ft. Collins, CO 80525
(303) 226-2504

OBJECTIVE
Chief Bank Examiner

PROFESSIONAL EXPERIENCE

CHIEF BANK EXAMINER   1984-present
<u>State of Colorado</u>

- Direct investigation of financial institutions for the State of Colorado to enforce laws and regulations governing establishment, operation, and solvency.

- Schedule audits according to departmental policy, availability of personnel, and financial condition of institution.

- Evaluate examination reports to determine action required to protect solvency of institution and interests of shareholders and depositors.

- Confer with financial advisors and other regulatory officials to recommend or initiate action against banks failing to comply with laws and regulations.

- Confer with officials of financial institutions industry to exchange views and discuss issues.

- Review application for merger, acquisition, establishment of new institution, acceptance in Federal Reserve System, and evaluate results of investigations undertaken to determine whether action is in public interest.

- Recommend acceptance or rejection of application on basis of findings.

EDUCATION
MBA, Business Administration, 1978
<u>University of Alabama at Birmingham</u>

BA, Accounting/Public Administration, 1974
<u>University of Denver</u>, Denver, CO

PREVIOUS EMPLOYMENT HISTORY
Senior Bank Examiner, <u>State of Alabama,</u> Birmingham, AL   1978-84
Staff Bank Examiner/Accountant, <u>State of Colorado</u>, Denver, CO   1974-78

GARRY STUART BLYE
213 Whitcomb Street
Ft. Collins, CO 80524
(303) 224-5432

OBJECTIVE
Chief Cost Estimator

PROFESSIONAL EXPERIENCE

CHIEF COST ESTIMATOR   1985-present
Hartley & Hartley Construction, Ft. Collins, CO

- Compile and analyze computerized data on all factors to survey costs before submitting bid proposals for future projects—materials, labor, location, and special machinery.

- Review architect's drawings, specifications, and other bidding documents.

- Visit the site of the proposed construction project to gather information and record in a signed report on access to the site and availability of electricity, water, and other services including topography and drainage.

- Determine the quantity of materials and labor, equipment, sequence of operations, and crew size needed.

- Analyze bids made by subcontractors.

- Write cost summary that includes cost of labor, equipment, materials, subcontracts, overhead, taxes, insurance, markup, and any other costs that affect the project.

- Prepare bid proposal for submission to the developer.

EDUCATION
MBA, Accounting, 1978
University of Alabama at Birmingham

BA, Accounting, 1974
University of Denver, Denver, CO

PREVIOUS EMPLOYMENT HISTORY
Cost Estimator, Allan Construction, Birmingham, AL   1976-85
Staff Cost Accountant, Design Property Management, Denver, CO   1974-76

AMANDA A. CRAWFORD
39804 Oceanana Place
Manhattan Beach, CA 90266
(213) 360-2250

PRESENTATION OF QUALIFICATIONS

Objective: Chief Financial Officer (CFO)

**QUALIFICATION
SUMMARY:** 16 years' experience in the Investment and Finance Industries. Strong emphasis on operations and reorganizational skills with the ability to rapidly analyze and recognize problems and opportunities. Successfully market products, services and concepts maintaining excellent customer and employee relations, resulting in production and profitability in highly competitive markets.

**PROFESSIONAL
EXPERIENCE:**

1986-present   **VICE PRESIDENT—FINANCE**, American Pension Consultants Inc, Los Angeles, CA. Managed entire operations involving $800K annual sales, reporting directly to the Board of Directors. Successfully designed and implemented investment advisory service. Established collective trusts with local bank involving hiring portfolio managers nationwide. Utilized research and marketing skills to evaluate portfolio managers and select effective performance monitoring system for collective trusts.

1982-86   **SENIOR FINANCIAL PLANNER/ANALYST**, Mary Selbert Inc, San Jose, CA. Provided computerized lease and real estate financial analysis on a time share basis working closely with commercial and investment bankers and brokers nationwide. Involved travel to major cities conducting presentations to market product strategies. Analyzed problem areas and successfully developed and implemented programs to improve operations. Increased sales from $2M to $6M, expanding its corporate staff and offices.

1972-82   **ASSISTANT PORTFOLIO MANAGER**, Louis & Co, San Francisco, CA. Liaison between investors, stockbrokers and bank officers. Researched and successfully solved problems for 30 portfolios; developed investment proposals and performance data for presentations.

EDUCATION: **MBA Degree - Management**, 1985
Golden Gate University, San Francisco, CA

BA Degree - Accounting
Miami University, Oxford, OH, 1971

CHARLES S. PRUETT
154 City Park Drive
Ft. Collins, CO 80524
(303) 224-5432

OBJECTIVE
Chief Financial Officer

PROFESSIONAL EXPERIENCE

CHIEF FINANCIAL OFFICER   1985-present
First Interstate Bank, Ft. Collins, CO
- Advise the President of this multimillion dollar financial institution in financial reporting, financial stability and liquidity and financial growth.

- Direct and supervise the work of the Controller, Treasurer and Internal Auditing Manager.

- Maintain close liaison and relationships with stockholders, financial institutions and the investment community.

- Serve on Board of Directors and Executive Committee and contribute in overall organizational planning, policy development and implementation.

PROFESSIONAL AFFILIATIONS
Member, American Accounting Association
Member, National Association of Finance Officers

EDUCATION
MBA, Accounting, 1971
California State University, Los Angeles

BA, Accounting, 1965
University of Denver, Denver, CO

PREVIOUS EMPLOYMENT HISTORY
Chief Financial Officer, Union Securities Corporation, Los Angeles, CA	1977-85
Treasurer, National Bank of Denver, Denver, CO	1971-77
Assistant Treasurer, Bank of Colorado, Ft. Collins, CO	1969-71
Treasury Operations Analyst, Bank of Colorado, Denver, CO	1966-69
Cash Management Staff Associate, Boise Bank & Trust, Boise, ID	1965-66

JOHN C. BLAKE
129 City Park Drive
Ft. Collins, CO 80524
(303) 224-0584

OBJECTIVE
A Hospital Controller position

PROFESSIONAL EXPERIENCE

CONTROLLER   1984-present
General Hospital, Denver, CO
* Manage the day-to-day financial operations of the hospital and assure that all financial transactions are properly recorded.
* Monitor and maintain compliance with federal and state regulations in regard to financial operations of the hospital.
* Maintain General ledgers and sub-systems.
* Prepare books for annual independent audit and supervise audit process.
* Implement and direct annual budget preparation between department managers and administration.
* Assist Treasurer of Hospital Board of Directors in maintaining appropriate cash flow for daily operations.
* Supervise specialists in third party reimbursement, cost reporting, and cost accounting.
* Interface with Human Resources on development and compliance with various hospital payroll/personnel policies.
* Direct hospital payroll processing to assure compliance with federal and state payroll laws.
* Coordinate reporting of financial information to outside agencies and organizations.
* Direct preparation of all hospital disbursements and verify documentation for proper approval.
* Provide assistance to the staff of the Foundation and General Hospital Homecare Service, Inc. to solve accounting problems.
* Direct preparation of monthly financial statements and document unusual occurrences and variances.
* Assist department managers with various financial related projects.

PROFESSIONAL AFFILIATIONS
Member, American Accounting Association
Member, Healthcare Financial Management Association

- More -

EDUCATION
MBA, Accounting, 1978
California State University, Los Angeles

BA, Accounting, 1971
University of Denver, Denver, CO

PREVIOUS EMPLOYMENT HISTORY

Assistant Controller, Valley Hospital, Los Angeles, CA   1978-84
General Accounting Manager, Poudre Homecare Svs., Ft. Collins, CO   1975-78
Staff Accountant, University Hospital, Denver, CO   1971-75

STEVEN L. YAKITORI
3201 Deer Run Court
Ft. Collins, CO 80525
(303) 223-0049

OBJECTIVE
A Controller position

PROFESSIONAL EXPERIENCE

CONTROLLER   1985-present
Poudre Valley Manufacturing Corporation, Ft. Collins, CO

- Direct financial activities of the manufacturing plant headquarters and two subdivisions of the organization.

- Delegate preparation of reports to management staff which summarize and forecast corporate business activity and financial position in areas of income, expenses, and earnings based on past, present and expected operations.

- Direct determination of depreciation rates to apply to capital assets.

- Establish and recommend to management, major economic objectives and policies for corporation and subdivisions.

- Direct preparation of budgets. Prepare reports required by regulatory agencies.

- Advise management on desirable operational adjustments due to tax code revisions and property and liability insurance coverage needed.

- Direct financial planning, procurement, and investment of funds for organization. Arrange for audits of accounts.

EDUCATION
MBA, Accounting, 1978
University of Hartford, CT

BA, Accounting, 1972
University of Denver, Denver, CO

PREVIOUS EMPLOYMENT HISTORY

Assistant Controller, Eastern Manufacturer Corporation, Hartford, CT	1978-85
Treasury Operation's Analyst, Financial Corporation, Denver, CO	1976-78
Staff-Cash Manager, World Banking Corporation, Denver, CO	1972-76

MICHAEL PAUL JOSEPH
12001 Stagecoach Road
Santa Barbara, CA 93110
(805) 966-0001

Objective: **Controller**

PROFESSIONAL EXPERIENCE

Cost Accounting
- Implement cost accounting systems.
  - Established complete integrated accounting package for entire corporations.
  - Tracked cost for multi-million dollar contracts.
  - Reduced costs for small businesses and large corporations.

Accounting & Budgeting
- Converted manual accounting systems to efficient computerized office systems for several companies throughout the Santa Barbara community.
  - Designed, installed and implemented effective budgeting systems under cash and accrual accounting methods.
  - Successfully tracked and reduced costs for multi-million dollar contracts.

Auditing
- Audited multi-million dollar subcontractors accounting records and facilities for government contracts.
- Analyzed problem areas and successfully developed programs to improve operations of local bank and entire restaurant chain.

Management & Administration
- Reported directly to the President. Accounting, Data Processing, Procurement Analysis & Review Departments reported directly to Controller.
  - Increased sales from $1M to $2.5M.
  - Hired, trained and supervised 2-40 employees.
  - Set up and conducted monthly motivational staff meetings.
- Established and implemented daily training programs to educate management and staff on new accounting office procedures.

EDUCATION
BA Degree, Business Economics, Accounting Emphasis
University of California at Santa Barbara, 1968

EMPLOYMENT HISTORY

Controller, ABC Business Inc, Santa Barbara, CA	1985-present
Assistant Controller, GDF Security Services Inc, Santa Barbara, CA	1978-85
Senior Accountant, DPZ Technology, Goleta, CA	1970-78

152

ARTHUR SAMUAL RAINIER
876 Rainier Court
Ventura, CA 93003
(805) 644-0009

Objective: A Controller position

PROFESSIONAL EXPERIENCE
Budgeting & Finance
- Prepared budgets and financial statements for real estate and engineering projects using a variety of computerized spreadsheet programs.
- Performed cost accounting analysis and produced work-in-progress variance reports for several operations levels.
- Monitored cost and schedule performance of technical programs for materials handling, accounting and individual projects throughout the company.
- Maintained an accounting software that issued reports to multiple departments.
- Set up and maintained a custom information retrieval system by integrating dBase III with the accounting software package.

Materials Management
- Established integrated purchasing and mfg. plans using MRP principals.
  - Set goals which reduced inventory levels and operating costs, resulting in 25 percent reduction in inventory and $20K reduction in labor costs.
  - Integrated production demands with purchasing and reduced stockouts.
  - Familiar with mil specs for parts, bills of material and quality assurance.
- Insured integrity of Master Parts list and Bills of Material for Configuration Control.
- Developed effective procedures for material handling—
  purchasing...receiving...stocking & inventory control...shipping.
- Supervised the flow of material through the production process in an engineer-to-order manufacturing operation.
- Thoroughly familiar with electronic components and mechanical assemblies.

EDUCATION
BA Degree, Accounting Emphasis, June 1983
University of California, Santa Barbara

EMPLOYMENT HISTORY
Material's Manager, The Research Laboratory, Goleta, CA   1986-present
Controller, The Linders Group, Santa Barbara, CA   1983-86

FREDRICK M. KILBRIDE
201 S. Lincoln
Ft. Collins, CO 80524
(303) 224-3340

OBJECTIVE
A Cost Accountant position

PROFESSIONAL EXPERIENCE

COST ACCOUNTANT   1985-present
Hewlett Packard Corporation, Loveland, CO

- Conduct studies which provide detailed cost information not supplied by general accounting systems:

  - Plan study and collect data to determine costs of business activities such as raw material purchases, inventory, and labor.

- Analyze computerized data obtained and record results.

- Developed and installed computer-based cost accounting system.

- Analyze changes in product design, raw materials, manufacturing methods, and services provided, to determine effects on costs.

- Provide management with reports specifying and comparing factors affecting prices and profitability of products and marketing support services.

- Analyze actual manufacturing costs and prepare periodic report comparing standard costs to actual production costs.

EDUCATION
MBA, Accounting, 1978
California State University, at Los Angeles

BA, Accounting, 1974
University of Denver, Denver, CO

PREVIOUS EMPLOYMENT HISTORY
Senior Accountant, Brigg's Engineering Corporation, Los Angeles, CA   1978-85
Staff Accountant, ABC Corporation, Denver, CO   1974-78

MICHAEL BRUCE BOLTON
125 County Road North
Ft. Collins, CO 80524
(303) 224-0549

OBJECTIVE
A Cost Accountant Management position

PROFESSIONAL EXPERIENCE

COST ACCOUNTANT MANAGER   1985-present
Ayla's Foods, Incorporated, Ft. Collins, CO
- Direct staff responsible for developing and modifying the cost accounting system for this multimillion dollar corporation.

- Develop product costing techniques and institute cost-control measures.

- Delegate detailed cost data, cost analysis, and report preparation to cost accounting staff.

- Make available timely and accurate labor, material, and overhead reports.

- Supervise the undertaking of special cost studies.

- Review allocation of overhead costs.

PROFESSIONAL AFFILIATIONS
Member, American Accounting Association
Member, Cost Management Group

EDUCATION
MBA, Accounting, 1978
University of Texas, Austin

BA, Accounting, 1974
University of Denver, Denver, CO

PREVIOUS EMPLOYMENT HISTORY
Senior Cost Accountant, General Foods Corporation, Austin, TX   1977-85
Staff Cost Accountant, Ayla's Foods, Corporation, Denver, CO   1974-77

JONATHAN T. HARVEST
123 City Park Drive
Ft. Collins, CO 80524
(303) 224-5439

OBJECTIVE
Cost Estimator

PROFESSIONAL EXPERIENCE

COST ESTIMATOR   1985-present
<u>Engineering High Technology</u>, Ft. Collins, CO

- Estimate costs associated with major redesign on existing products and development of new products in the production process.
- Review blueprints or conceptual drawings to determine the machining operations, tools and gauges, and materials required for each job.
- Prepare a parts list and determine whether it is more efficient to produce or to purchase parts.
- Initiate inquiries for price information from potential suppliers and cost of manufacturing for each component of the product.
- Determine cost of software for the massive amounts of computer programming involved in most projects during the design stage.
- Prepare time-phase charts and problem-elimination learning curves to indicate the time required for tool design and fabrication, tool "debugging," manufacturing of parts, assembly, and testing.
- Calculate the standard labor hours necessary to produce a predetermined number of units. Convert into dollar values and add factors for waste, overhead, and profit to yield the unit cost in dollars.
- Compare the cost of purchasing parts with the firm's cost of manufacturing to determine the most cost effective price.
- Use computerized estimates for complex mathematical techniques—parametric analysis.

EDUCATION
MBA, Accounting, 1978
<u>University of Alabama at Birmingham</u>

BA, Accounting, 1971
<u>University of Denver</u>, Denver, CO

PREVIOUS EMPLOYMENT HISTORY
Cost Estimator, <u>Applied Computer Technology</u>, Birmingham, AL   1974-85
Cost Accountant, <u>Jared Engineering Concepts</u>, Denver, CO   1971-74

MAX J. HOLDEN
2145 Terry Shores Drive
Ft. Collins, CO 80524
(303) 224-5612

OBJECTIVE
Credit Analysis Manager

PROFESSIONAL EXPERIENCE

CREDIT ANALYSIS MANAGER   1985-present
United Bank of Ft. Collins, Ft. Collins, CO

- Direct credit analysis personnel in collection follow-up, operations and management of credit approval practices.

- Provide detailed analysis of collection/audit activity to upper management.

- Set standards to be followed in granting credit and collecting.

PROFESSIONAL AFFILIATIONS
Member, American Accounting Association
Member, American Institute of Certified Public Accountants

EDUCATION
MBA, Accounting, 1978
California State University, Los Angeles

BA, Accounting, 1972
University of Denver, Denver, CO

PREVIOUS EMPLOYMENT HISTORY
Senior Credit Analyst, Security Pacific National Bank, Los Angeles, CA   1977-85
Credit Analyst, Financial Mortgage Corporation, Denver, CO   1974-77
Staff Accountant, Charles & Associates, Denver, CO   1972-74

HERSCHEL S. SAPIR
901 Whedbee Street
Ft. Collins, CO 80524
(303) 224-5439

OBJECTIVE
A Credit Analyst Management position

PROFESSIONAL EXPERIENCE
SENIOR CREDIT ANALYST
University Bank of Colorado, Ft. Collins, CO   1984-present
- Analyze credit information to determine risk involved in lending money to commercial customers, and prepare report of findings.

- Select information, including company financial statements and balance sheet and record data on computerized spreadsheet.

- Enter codes for computer program to generate ratios for use in evaluating commercial customer's financial status.

- Compare liquidity, profitability, credit history, and cash, with other companies of same industry, size, and geographic location.

- Analyze income growth, quality of management, market share, potential risks of industry, and collateral appraisal.

- Write loan application/offering sheet and results of credit analysis and summary of loan request. Describe credit risk and amount of loan profit.

- Submit offering sheet to loan committee for decision.

- Visit companies to collect information as part of analysis.

- Train and supervise interns and new credit analyst staff members.

EDUCATION
MBA, Accounting, 1978
University of Hartford, CT

BA, Accounting, 1974
University of Denver, Denver, CO

PREVIOUS EMPLOYMENT HISTORY
Credit Analyst, United Bank of Hartford, Hartford, CT   1976-84

MARIAN J. HARVEY
3039 City Park Drive
Ft. Collins, CO 80524
(303) 224-0934

OBJECTIVE
Senior Credit Counselor

PROFESSIONAL EXPERIENCE
CREDIT COUNSELOR
<u>Credit Counseling Services of Colorado</u>, Ft. Collins, CO   1985-present
- Licensed by the State of Colorado to provide financial counseling to individuals in debt.

- Confer with client to ascertain available monthly income after living expenses to meet credit obligations.

- Calculate amount of debt and funds available to plan method of payoff and estimate time for debt liquidation.

- Contact creditors to explain client's financial situation; arrange for payment adjustments so payments are feasible for client and agreeable to creditors.

- Establish payment priorities to reduce client's overall costs by liquidating high-interest, short-term loans or contracts first.

- Open account for client and disburse funds from account to creditors as agent for client.

- Keep records of account activity.

- Counsel client on personal and family financial problems, such as excessive spending and borrowing of funds.

EDUCATION
MBA, Business Administration, 1978
<u>University of Hartford, CT</u>

BA, Accounting, 1974
<u>University of Denver</u>, Denver, CO

PREVIOUS EMPLOYMENT HISTORY
Credit Counselor, <u>Credit Counseling Services of Hartford</u>, Hartford, CT   1978-85
Credit Counselor, <u>Denver Credit Counseling Service</u>, Denver, CO   1974-78

GEORGE SAUL WEISS
232 City Park Drive
Denver, CO 80555
(303) 223-0498

OBJECTIVE
Director of Underwriter Solicitation

PROFESSIONAL EXPERIENCE

DIRECTOR, UNDERWRITER
Public Television Broadcasting   1985-present
• Plan and direct activities to secure and maintain funding of public television.

• Review reports, periodicals, and other materials to identify prospective funding sources for proposed broadcast programs.

• Direct and counsel subordinates in developing strategies to secure program funding and negotiate final agreements with funding establishment representatives.

• Serve as liaison between station's legal, programming, public information, and other departmental staff and funding business personnel to provide information on status of projects and to resolve problems.

• Specialize in solicitation of funding from government, foundation, and corporation sources.

EDUCATION
MBA, Business Administration, 1978
University of Hartford, CT

BA, Accounting, 1974
University of Denver, Denver, CO

PREVIOUS EMPLOYMENT HISTORY
Underwriter, Public Broadcast Corporation, Hartford, CT   1980-85
Internal Auditor Manager, KTCR Radio, Hartford, CT   1977-80
Internal Auditor, Public Television Broadcasting, Denver, CO   1974-77

BRADLEY S. CHINOOK
2145 Stuart Street
Ft. Collins, CO 80524
(303) 224-0548

OBJECTIVE
Director of Utility Accounts

PROFESSIONAL EXPERIENCE

DIRECTOR, UTILITY ACCOUNTS
City of Ft. Collins, Ft. Collins, CO   1984-present

- Evaluate financial condition of electric, telephone, gas, water, and public transit utility companies to facilitate work of regulatory commissions in setting rules.

- Analyze annual reports, financial statements, and other records submitted by utility companies, applying accepted accounting and statistical analysis procedures to determine current financial condition.

- Evaluate reports from commission staff members and field investigators regarding condition of company property and other factors influencing solvency and profitability.

- Prepare and present exhibits and testify during commission hearings on regulatory or rate adjustments.

- Confer with company officials to discuss financial problems and regulatory matters.

- Direct workers engaged in filing company financial records.

- Conduct specialized studies, such as cost of service, revenue requirement, and cost allocation studies for commission, or design new rates in accordance with findings of commission.

EDUCATION
MBA, Public Administration, 1978
University of Hartford, CT

BA, Accounting, 1974
University of Denver, Denver, CO

PREVIOUS EMPLOYMENT HISTORY
Utility Accounts Manager, City of Hartford, Hartford, CT   1978-84
Accountant, City of Denver, Denver, CO   1974-78

DAPHNEY MACMURRY
225 Woodridge Road
Montecito, CA 93108
(805) 685-4231

FINANCIAL ACCOUNT EXECUTIVE

PROFESSIONAL OBJECTIVE:

Seeking a progressive company with innovative products, salary and commission with unlimited earning potential.

PROFESSIONAL PROFILE:

Success oriented with high energy and a positive attitude. outstanding talent for assessing client's needs...communicate effectively with all levels of management in a highly professional and diplomatic manner...problem solver and team player with ability to work independently...enthusiastic, creative and flexible.

SALES EXPERIENCE WITH PROVEN TRACK RECORD:

1989-present

ACCOUNT EXECUTIVE
Call America Business Inc, Santa Barbara, CA. Sell a wide range of long distance services to commercial accounts in Santa Barbara. Demonstrate effective cold calling, appointment setting and follow up. Deliver dynamic product presentations and write effective proposals. Identify clients' needs, problems and solutions through long distance analysis. Became #1 sales rep. in the first year through assertive sales ability, thorough product knowledge and consistent follow up.

1987-89

COMMODITY BROKER (AP)
West Coast Commodities Corporation, Santa Barbara, CA. Directly involved in buying and selling commodities, specializing in options. Maintained existing equity and client contact. Emphasis on telemarketing sales to raise equity for existing book. Developed and instructed sales training programs monitoring motivational meetings for sales staff.

EDUCATION:

BA Degree, Business Economics, 1987
University of California at Santa Barbara

KEVIN ALLEN BRADY
67716 Loma Linda Road
Santa Barbara, CA 93103
(805) 569-0003

Objective: International Finance Advisor/Manager

PROFILE:
- Two years' working experience in banking and int'l business.
- Business Translator for <u>Veneconomia</u>, a business journal.
- <u>Computer skills</u>: Lotus 1-2-3, dBase III and Word Perfect.
- <u>Tri-lingual</u>: Highly proficient in Spanish and French.

EXPERIENCE:

1988-present   **FINANCIAL ADVISOR**, <u>Petroltubos, SA</u>, Caracus, Venezuela
- Translated technical documents.
- Calculated business market value; projected/analyzed cash flow.
- Designed a program to automatically calculate sale prices.
- Prepared briefs analyzing the different areas of the company.
- Designed programs to organize depreciation and imports.

Summer-1988   **MERCHANT BANKING INTERN**, <u>Banque de Groof</u>, Brussels, Belgium
- Translated economic and legal documents.
- Evaluated performance on pension fund management.
- Researched and wrote Venture Capital report.
- Calculated the return on funds managed according to the dividend discount model.

Spring-1988   **INT'L TRADE INTERN**, <u>Arizona Dept of Commerce</u>, Phoenix, **AZ**
- Wrote a speech for an Arizona business conference on the "International Trade, The Falling Dollar and Third World Debt."
- Wrote a speech for Asian-American conference on "The Role of Asian-Americans in United States-Asia Trade."
- Designed economic/political country briefs.

1983-84   **CORPORATE ENGLISH TEACHER**
<u>Instituto de Loesher</u>, Caracas, Venezuela
- Taught English lessons to corporate groups.

EDUCATION:
Master of International Management
<u>American Graduate School</u>, 1988
Thunderbird Campus, Glendale, AZ

Bachelor of Arts, Finance, 1983
<u>University of California</u>, Santa Barbara

DAVID ALLAN QUINCY
PO Box 123
Los Angeles, CA 90067
(213) 987-1234

Objective: A Financial Analyst position with an International Lender

PROFESSIONAL EXPERIENCE

Financial Management
- Founded with two other members, a software company which developed a system for institutions trading foreign exchange and related instruments.
  - Gathered information and made strategic decisions concerning target markets, advertising and company direction.
  - Achieved sales of $400K in the company's initial year.
  - Designed and implemented enhancements for proprietary system, working closely with traders and systems personnel.
  - Wrote promotional literature and client training manual.
  - Set up company accounting books and procedures.
- Managed the credit department of a corporate bank branch in Spain.
  - Analyzed loan proposals, and recommended decisions for approval.
  - Prepared accounting functions and monitored existing loan portfolio.
- Supervised a staff of 15 employees for a bank branch in Spain.
  - Met target levels resulting in profits of $100K per month.

Research Analysis & Evaluation
- Participated in the development of a financial analysis package to be used throughout the bank worldwide.
  - One of two junior officers chosen for the bank's internal consulting cell.
- Created a highly sophisticated system for tracking prospective clients.
- Selected to revise countrywide marketing strategies throughout Spain, working directly with the General Manager.
- Received "A" rating for performance in the academic bank training program.

EDUCATION
MBA Candidate, Emphasis: Finance & Int'l Business
The Anderson School of Management at UCLA

BS Degree, Economics, Emphasis: Finance   May 1984
The Wharton School of the University of Pennsylvania

EMPLOYMENT HISTORY

Manager/Lending Officer, Bank of Commerce Espanola, Spain	1986-present
Junior Officer, Bank of Commerce International, London, England	1985-86
Management Trainee, Bank of Commerce International, New York, NY	1984-85
Co-Founder, Bundy Software, Inc, Los Angeles, CA	1980-84

SAM LUCAS CRAFTON
8872 Steamboat Lane
Boulder, CO 80205
(303) 492-0009

OBJECTIVE
A Financial Corporate Trainer position

PROFESSIONAL EXPERIENCE
Financial Training Support
- Pioneered expansion for a major Wall Street firm from 43 to 180 sales offices nationwide.
- Identified, selected and educated mid-level and senior-level executives to provide retirement planning for employees of non-profit organizations.
- Developed highly successful marketing strategies and workshops for promotions.
  - Established modular training for 500 Registered Benefit Specialists.
  - Conducted motivational and education workshops.
  - Identified prospective clients; trained personnel to enroll clients.
  - Supervised and monitored programs on-location nationwide.

Sales/Management Experience
- Developed a unique retirement planning concept for employees of non-profit organizations, corporations and self-employed individuals.
  - Identified, selected, trained and supported registered sales representatives.
  - Delivered weekly motivational sales and educational staff meetings.
  - Supported regional, divisional and registered representatives in the field.
- Achieved top 3% of companies $4 billion in assets through excellent sales ability, thorough product knowledge and superior customer service.

EDUCATION
BBA, University of New York
Certified Financial Planner, 1974

PROFESSIONAL AFFILIATIONS
Board of Directors:
International Association. for Financial Planning
Certified Financial Planning Program, University of New York
Chamber of Commerce, Denver, CO
Sales & Marketing Executive Club, Denver, CO
President/Chairman, IAFP, Denver, CO

EMPLOYMENT HISTORY
Financial Advisor, Investors Management Corp, Denver, CO   1986-present
Sales Manager, The Investors Corporation, NY, NY   1972-86

JUDY ANNE JORDAN
2391 West Mulberry Street
Ft. Collins, CO 80524
(303) 224-3314

OBJECTIVE
Financial Planning Manager

PROFESSIONAL EXPERIENCE

FINANCIAL PLANNING MANAGER   1985-present
University Bank, Ft. Collins, CO
• Delegate financial and budget analysis functions including profit planning,
  capital expenditures, investments, cash flow budgeting and acquisitions to
  financial planning personnel.

• Perform financial/economic analyses of new projects and analyses of merger
  and corporate growth policies.

• Hire, train, and supervise financial planning staff.

PROFESSIONAL AFFILIATIONS
Member, American Accounting Association
Member, American Institute of Financial Planners

EDUCATION
MBA, Accounting, 1978
California State University, Los Angeles

BA, Accounting, 1974
University of Denver, Denver, CO

PREVIOUS EMPLOYMENT HISTORY
Financial Planning Supervisor, First Interstate Bank, Los Angeles, CA   1977-85
Financial Planner, United Bank of Denver, Denver, CO   1974-77

SUSAN LUANNE WEINSTEIN
1432 Laport Avenue
Ft. Collins, CO 80524
(303) 224-0548

OBJECTIVE
Financial Management Systems Analyst

PROFESSIONAL EXPERIENCE
FINANCIAL MANAGEMENT ANALYST   1984-present
The Wyatt Corporation, Ft. Collins, CO

- Analyze financial operating procedures to devise most efficient methods of accomplishing work for corporate headquarters with five subdivisions.

- Plan study of work problems and procedures inventory control, cost analysis, information flow, and integrated production methods.

- Gather and organize information on possible problems, including present financial operating procedures.

- Analyze data gathered, develop information and consider available solutions or alternate methods of proceeding.

- Organize and document findings of studies and prepare recommendations for implementation of new finance systems, procedures or organizational changes.

- Confer with personnel to assure smooth functioning of newly implemented systems.

- Install new financial systems and train personnel in application.

- Conduct operational effectiveness reviews to ensure project systems are applied and functioning as designed.

- Develop and update operational manuals outlining established methods of performing work in accordance with policy.

EDUCATION
MBA, Computer Science, 1978
University of Hartford, CT

BA, Accounting, 1972
University of Denver, Denver, CO

PREVIOUS EMPLOYMENT HISTORY
Systems Analyst, Colorado State University, Ft. Collins, CO   1978-84
Staff Accountant, University of Denver, Finance Department   1972-76

RYLAND DORSEY
519 W. Alamar #12
Houston, TX 93105
(801) 224-6785

Objective: A Financial Management Consultant

PROFESSIONAL PROFILE:
- Success oriented and outgoing with a positive attitude
- Strong sense of responsibility and self motivation
- Good written, oral and interpersonal communication skills
- Problem solver and team player with proven leadership qualities
- Rapidly analyze and recognize problems and find solutions
- Strong organizational skills with attention to detail
- Creative, flexible and efficient work habits.
- Thorough knowledge of developing company cross training programs.

PROFESSIONAL EXPERIENCE:

Denver, Management Services, Denver, CO   1990-present
Financial Management Consultant
- Analyzed departments needs and designed systems and procedures.
- Set up workshops and trained new policy/procedures to employees.
- Designed mini computer systems, wrote requests for proposals.
- Evaluated and selected vendors to purchase hardware and software.
- Worked with vendors to design custom software to meet their specific needs.
- Developed seminars to prepare employees for training on computer.
- Trained/cross trained entire company all phases of computer system.

EDUCATION:
MA Degree - Business Economics, 1979
Antioch University, Houston, TX

BS Degree - Computer Science, 1975
Western Washington University, Bellingham, WA

EMPLOYMENT HISTORY:
Consultant, Houston Computer Corp, Houston, TX   1986-89
Consultant, Puget Sound Company, Seattle, WA   1983-86
Systems Mgr, KD Engineering, Seattle, WA   1979-83

RAMONA S. RAMIREZ
321 Whedbee Street
Ft. Collins, CO 80524
(303) 224-5945

OBJECTIVE
Finance Manager

PROFESSIONAL EXPERIENCE

MANAGER OF FINANCE 1985-present
Microcomputer Products Corporation, Ft. Collins, CO

- Wrote a business plan which qualified the company for a government grant for industries impacted by imports to develop a new computer system.

- Motivated research and development staff to perform in a turn-around situation at below their earning capabilities.

- Settled all lawsuits and negotiated with creditors in discounting payables and deferring payments.

- Generated a positive cash flow by reducing overhead costs, accelerating collections and converting excess inventory and assets into cash.

- Improved relations with dealers and used their input to formulate company's plans for developing a market-oriented product.

- Implemented preparation of inventory control and asset counts, payroll, sales, property tax forms.

- Analyzed and prepared financial statements; updated product costs and budget variances.

- Managed an accounting staff of 18 employees.

EDUCATION
MBA, Accounting, 1978
California State University, Los Angeles

BA, Accounting, 1972
University of Denver, Denver, CO

PREVIOUS EMPLOYMENT HISTORY
Senior Cost Accountant, Magnetic Computer Corp., Los Angeles, CA   1976-85
Cost Accountant, Mercer Computer Corporation, Denver, CO   1972-76

HENRY CHARLES NOWAK
1237 Terry Lake Drive
Ft. Collins, CO 80524
(303) 224-9584

OBJECTIVE
Financial Services Sales Representative

PROFESSIONAL EXPERIENCE

UNIVERSITY BANK, Ft. Collins, CO   1985-present
Financial Services Sales Representative
- Sell financial services to customers of the bank.
- Develop prospects from current commercial customers, referral leads, and other sources.
- Contact prospective customers to present information on available services: deposit accounts, line-of-credit, sales or inventory financing, cash management, and investment services.
- Determine customers' financial service needs and prepare proposal to sell services.
- Review business trends and advise customers regarding expected fluctuations.
- Attend sales and trade meetings to develop new business prospects.
- Conduct presentations on financial services to groups to attract new clients.
- Prepare agreement to complete sale.
- Evaluate costs and revenue of agreements to determine if they are profitable enough to continue.
- Sell services to other financial institutions: check processing and collecting, record keeping and reporting, trust, investment, safekeeping services, and travelers checks.
- Solicit businesses to participate in consumer credit card program.

EDUCATION
MBA, Accounting, 1978
California State University, Los Angeles

BA, Accounting, 1974
University of Denver, Denver, CO

PREVIOUS EMPLOYMENT HISTORY
Financial Planner, Bank of A. Levy, Ventura, CA   1978-85
Financial Planner, Bank of Colorado, Denver, CO   1974-78

DAPHNE CAROLINE SCHMIDT
6904 West Elizabeth
Ft. Collins, CO 80521
(303) 224-5430

OBJECTIVE
A General Accounting Manager position

PROFESSIONAL EXPERIENCE

Senior General Accountant   1986-present
Applied Magnetics Corporation, Denver, CO

- Direct and coordinate activities of other accountants and clerical workers performing accounting and bookkeeping tasks.

- Establish, modify, document, and coordinate implementation of accounting and accounting control procedures.

- Devise and implement computer-based system for general accounting.

- Analyze financial information and prepare financial reports.

- Compile and analyze financial information to prepare entries to general ledger accounts and documenting business transactions.

- Analyze financial information detailing assets, liabilities, and capital, and prepare balance sheet, profit and loss statement, and other reports to summarize current and projected corporate financial position using the computer.

- Audit contracts, orders, and vouchers, and prepare reports to substantiate individual transactions prior to settlement.

EDUCATION
BBA, Accounting, 1978
University of Texas at Austin

PREVIOUS EMPLOYMENT HISTORY
Staff General Accountant, Shell Western Oil, Houston, TX   1978-86
Accounting Intern, Austin Corporation, Austin, TX   Summers 1975-78

SUZANNE S. STEWART
4807 Coldwater Canyon
Studio City, CA 94123
(818) 366-5435

OBJECTIVE
General Accounting Manager

PROFESSIONAL EXPERIENCE

GENERAL ACCOUNTANT
University Hospital, Los Angeles, CA   1988-present
- Interpret Medicare regulations and publications, prepare Medicare cost reports and audit, and calculate write-offs.
- Monitor provider based physicians and their contracts.
- Develop, maintain and update standard costs for computerized cost accounting.
- Reconcile year-end accounts receivable.
- Supervise and train employees on the cost accounting system.
- Develop Patient Days worksheet and distribute on a timely basis.
- Monitor and report the pass-through payments to the Intermediary.
- Calculate Case Mix Index and adjust through Intermediary for changes in payment rate.
- Approve and monitor new billing procedures and charge changes.
- Assist budget analyst with budget preparation.

PROFESSIONAL AFFILIATIONS
Member, American Accounting Association

EDUCATION
MBA, Accounting, 1990
California State University, Los Angeles

BA, Accounting, 1980
University of Denver, Denver, CO

PREVIOUS EMPLOYMENT HISTORY
General Accountant, General Hospital, Denver, CO   1985-88
General Accountant, Children's Hospital, Denver, CO   1980-85

ROBERT C. COSTIC, C.P.A.
890 West Mulberry Street
Ft. Collins, CO 80524
(303) 224-5432

OBJECTIVE
General Accountant Manager

PROFESSIONAL EXPERIENCE

GENERAL ACCOUNTANT MANAGER   1985-present
The Wyatt Corporation
- Assist controller with financial accounting and budgetary planning and control functions.

- In charge of coordinating and directing detailed accounting entries including receivables, payables, payroll, property, and general ledger to general accounting staff.

- Delegate internal financial reporting and financial statements to general accounting staff.

PROFESSIONAL AFFILIATIONS
Member, American Accounting Association
Member, American Institute of Certified Public Accountants

EDUCATION
MBA, Accounting, 1978
California State University, Los Angeles

BA, Accounting, 1974
University of Denver, Denver, CO

PREVIOUS EMPLOYMENT HISTORY
Sr. General Accountant, Abbott Ford Enterprises, Los Angeles, CA   1977-85
General Accountant, R & R Corporation, Denver, CO   1974-77

DONALD S. TARMIGAN
326 Terry Point Drive
Ft. Collins, CO 80524
(303) 224-5041

OBJECTIVE
Internal Audit Manager

PROFESSIONAL EXPERIENCE

INTERNAL AUDIT MANAGER   1985-present
Fornie Industries, Ft. Collins, CO
- Direct responsibilities to auditing staff to ensure adequacy and reliability of the internal control systems.

- Conduct statistical samples of document approval.

- Perform special tests to uncover defalcations.

- Perform operational audits for profit improvement recommendations. Make recommendations for changes.

- Insure that company policies and procedures are followed and establish the proper techniques to discover and prevent fraud.

- Select areas of concern for operational auditing.

PROFESSIONAL AFFILIATIONS
Member, American Accounting Association
Member, Institute of Internal Auditors

EDUCATION
MBA, Accounting, 1978
California State University, Los Angeles

BA, Accounting, 1974
University of Denver, Denver, CO

PREVIOUS EMPLOYMENT HISTORY
Senior Internal Auditor, Jerod High Technology, Los Angeles, CA   1981-85
Internal Auditor, Medicon Medical Services, Denver, CO   1974-81

GEOFFREY TRAVIS WAYLAND

2093 W. Mulberry Street
Ft. Collins, CO 80525
(303) 224-0594

OBJECTIVE
An Internal Auditor Manager position

PROFESSIONAL EXPERIENCE

INTERNAL AUDITOR, SR.   1985-present
City of Denver, Denver, CO

- Conduct audits for management to assess effectiveness of controls, accuracy of financial records, and efficiency of operations.

- Examine records of departments and interview workers to ensure recording of transactions and compliance with applicable laws and regulations.

- Inspect accounting systems to determine their efficiency and protective value.

- Review records pertaining to material assets, including equipment and buildings, and staff to determine degree to which they are utilized.

- Analyze data obtained for evidence of deficiencies in controls, duplication of effort, extravagance, fraud, or lack of compliance with laws, government regulations, and management policies.

- Prepare reports of findings and recommendations for management staff.

- Conduct special studies for management to detect fraud and to develop controls for fraud prevention.

- Audit employer business records to determine unemployment insurance premiums, liabilities, and employer compliance with state tax laws.

EDUCATION
MBA, Accounting, 1978
University of Alabama at Birmingham

BA, Accounting, 1974
University of Denver, Denver, CO

PREVIOUS EMPLOYMENT HISTORY

Internal Auditor, City of Birmingham, AL   1978-85
Internal Auditor, City of Loveland, Golden, CO   1974-78

IRA B. ISRAEL
1290 Mathews Street
Ft. Collins, CO 80524
(303) 224-5443

OBJECTIVE
A Portfolio Management position

PROFESSIONAL EXPERIENCE

SENIOR INVESTMENT ANALYST
Denver Securities Corporation, Denver, CO   1985-present

- Analyze financial information to forecast business, industry, and economic conditions, for use in making investment decisions to purchase bonds, commodities, equity, currency and portfolio management.

- Gather and analyze company financial states, industry, regulatory and economic information, and financial periodicals and newspapers.

- Interpret data concerning price, yield, stability, and future trends of investments.

- Summarize data describing current and long term trends in investment risks and economic influences pertinent to investments.

- Draw computerized charts and graphs to illustrate reports.

- Recommend investment timing and buy-and-sell orders to company or to staff of investments establishment for advising clients.

- Call brokers and purchase investments for company.

- Recommend modifications to management's investment policy.

EDUCATION
MBA, Business Economics, 1978
University of Alabama at Birmingham

BA, Accounting, 1974
University of Denver, Denver, CO

PREVIOUS EMPLOYMENT HISTORY
Securities Analyst, Birmingham Investor's Corporation, Birmingham, AL   1976-85
Securities-Research Analyst, STP Portfolio Management, Denver, CO   1974-76

STUART B. SMITH
430 Fresno Way
Ft. Collins, CO 80524
(303) 224-5340

OBJECTIVE
An Investment Executive position

PROFESSIONAL EXPERIENCE

INVESTMENT EXECUTIVE   1985-present
SPT Financial Services, Ft. Collins, CO
- Sell financial products and services to clients for investment purposes, applying knowledge of securities, investment plans, market conditions and regulations.

- Identify and solicit business from potential clients.

- Interview clients to determine financial position, resources, assets available to invest, and financial goals.

- Provide clients with information and advice on purchase or sale of securities, financial services, and investment plans, based on review of professional publications and knowledge of securities market and financial service industry.

- Complete sales order tickets and submit tickets to support personnel for processing of client requested transaction.

- Read status reports, perform calculations to monitor client accounts and verify transactions.

LICENSE
Series 7 License: 1974

EDUCATION
MBA, Accounting, 1978
California State University, Los Angeles

BA, Accounting, 1974
University of Denver, Denver, CO

PREVIOUS EMPLOYMENT HISTORY
Sr. Financial Planner, World Bank, Los Angeles, CA   1978-85
Financial Planner, Bank of Denver, Denver, CO   1974-78

KEVIN BLACK
3848 Goshen Avenue
Ft. Collins, CO 80524
(303) 224-3049

OBJECTIVE
A Management position with a Financial Institution

PROFESSIONAL EXPERIENCE

Financial Management
- Founder of an international corporation that developed a system for institutions to trade foreign exchange and related instruments.
- Gathered information and made strategic decisions concerning target markets, advertising, and company direction.
- Achieved sales of $400K in the company's first year.
- Designed and implemented enhancements for clients' computerized accounting systems.
- Wrote promotional literature and client training manual.
- Set up the corporation's accounting systems and procedures.
- Managed the credit department of a corporate bank branch in Spain and met target levels resulting in profits of $100K per month.
- Analyzed loan proposals, and recommended decisions for approval.
- Prepared accounting functions and monitored existing loan portfolio.
- Supervised a staff of 15 employees.

Financial Analysis & Evaluation
- Participated in developing a financial analysis package to be used throughout the bank worldwide.
- Created a highly sophisticated system for tracking prospective client contacts, working closely with traders and systems personnel.
- Selected to revise marketing strategies throughout Spain.

EDUCATION
MBA, Candidate, Emphasis: Finance & Int'l Business
The Anderson School of Management at UCLA

BA, Accounting, 1984
University of Denver, Denver, CO

EMPLOYMENT HISTORY
Founder, Zaitech Corporation, New York, NY   1988-92
Lending Officer/Manager, Bank of Credit & Commerce Espanola, Spain   1986-88
Junior Officer, Bank of Credit & Commerce Int'l, London, England   1985-86
Management Trainee, Bank of Credit & Commerce Int'l, New York, NY   1984-85

JENNA LEIGH SONNEBURG
1134 Peacock Lane
Santa Barbara, CA 93103
(805) 569-2222

OBJECTIVE
A Senior Loan Officer Position

PROFESSIONAL EXPERIENCE
BANK OF SANTA BARBARA, Santa Barbara, CA   1969-present
Senior Loan Officer

Training, Management & Administration
- Trained/supervised loan and operation staff at branch offices throughout Santa Barbara.
  - Successfully set up and managed the Home Loan Center in Ventura for one year.
  - Supervised and cross-trained operations staff of 6-20 employees for six years.
  - Became main source of information for in-house loan officers in Santa Barbara.
  - Converted manual procedures to an effective in-house computerized office system.
  - Enforce policies & regulations, meeting daily demanding deadline schedules.
  - Develop and conduct effective policy and operation training seminars and presentations to the general public, real estate offices and in-house loan officers throughout Santa Barbara Tri-county areas.
- Prepare and monitor monthly reports and primary banking functions.
- Developed and designed original tracking reports now used to follow all loans.

Accounting & Cash Management
- Consistently funded monthly loans totalling over $1M, receiving numerous awards.
- Analyze problem areas and successfully develop and implement programs to improve operations and produce profits.
  - Analyze credit histories and cash flow projections to determine loan requirements.
  - Effectively counsel, evaluate and inform customers of credit options for wise long and short term investments.
- Monitor cash requirements for the entire bank.

SPECIAL SKILLS
Cash handling, stop payments, returned checks, forgeries, fund posting, employee and depositor inquiries, process complex transactions, prepare financial records, supervise preparation of reviews, reconcile and verify monthly reports and investment portfolio accounting, statement preparation, posting/redemption of bonds, prepare/maintain detailed operating procedures, operate computers.

EDUCATION
BA Degree, Business Economics, 1969
University of California, Los Angeles

MARK B. REDDIE
3234 Whitcomb Street
Ft. Collins, CO 80524
(303) 224-4503

OBJECTIVE
A Management Services Consultant Manager position

PROFESSIONAL EXPERIENCE

SENIOR MANAGEMENT SERVICE CONSULTING STAFF   1985-present
Arthur Anderson, Denver, CO

- Supervise detailed consulting assignments involving various functional areas within client organization; computing, personnel, marketing.

- Devise and install customized automated accounting systems and related procedures for businesses worldwide.

- Conduct survey of operations to ascertain corporate needs.

- Set up classification of accounts and organize accounting procedures and machine methods support.

- Devise forms and prepare manuals required to guide activities of bookkeeping and clerical personnel who post data and keep records.

EDUCATION

MBA, Accounting, 1978
California State University, at Los Angeles

BA, Computer Science, 1974
University of California at Los Angeles

PREVIOUS EMPLOYMENT HISTORY

Management Services Consultant, Arthur Anderson, Los Angeles, CA   1980-85
Computer Programmer, IBM Corporation, Los Angeles, CA   1974-80

CYNTHIA MEGAN KANTWELL
369 Pacific Coast Highway
Malibu, CA 90265
(213) 971-4443

OBJECTIVE

A challenging career in **Portfolio Management**

PROFESSIONAL PROFILE

- Valuable business contacts in the bond market worldwide.
- Extensive knowledge of financial instruments.
- Thrive on new opportunities for accomplishment and success.
- Sharp analytic, problem solving and presentation skills.
- Work well under highly pressured situations.
- Special talent for understanding client needs.

PROFESSIONAL EXPERIENCE

LOS ANGELES FIXED INCOME MANAGEMENT, Beverly Hills, CA   1982-present
Principal & Portfolio Manager/Trader

Portfolio Management
- Manage $5 billion of total-rate-of-return fixed income portfolios:
  - Long duration...short duration...taxable...tax-exempt...sterling...individuals...nuclear decommissioning...immunization funds.
- Implement a highly disciplined investment process, flexible under all market conditions.
- In charge of active trading room and corresponding settlement operations.

Trading
- Maintain critical mode of evaluating and analyzing fixed income investment instruments and strategies.
- Analyze and trade various fixed income securities:
  Governments...municipals...foreigns...corporates...mortgages.
- Evaluate yield curves, currencies, option adjusted spreads, duration and convexity.

Research Analysis & Evaluation
- Established an efficient credit research system.
- Organize client goals, objectives and restrictions.
- Monitor client characteristics.

EDUCATION

BA Degree, Business Economics, 1982
University of California, Los Angeles

GARRY STEFAN YORK
1209 Loveland Lane
Ft. Collins, CO 80525
(303) 226-0034

OBJECTIVE
A Revenue Agent position

PROFESSIONAL EXPERIENCE
REVENUE AGENT
Internal Revenue Service, Ft. Collins, CO   1986-present
- Conduct independent field audits and investigations of federal income tax returns to verify or amend tax liabilities of business throughout Larimer County.

- Examine tax returns to determine nature and extent of audits to be performed.

- Analyze accounting books and records to determine appropriateness of accounting methods employed and compliance with statutory provisions.

- Investigate documents, financial transactions, operation methods, industry practices and legal instruments, to develop information regarding inclusiveness of accounting records and tax returns.

- Confer with taxpayer or representative to explain issues involved and applicability of pertinent tax laws and regulations.

- Secure taxpayer's agreement to discharge tax assessment or submit contested determination to other administrative or judicial conferees for appeals hearings.

- Participate in formal appeals hearings on contested cases from other agents.

- Serve as member of regional appeals board to reexamine unresolved issues in terms of relevant laws and regulations.

EDUCATION
MBA, Public Administration, 1978
University of Hartford, Hartford, CT

BA, Business Economics, Accounting Emphasis, 1974
University of California, Santa Barbara, CA

PREVIOUS EMPLOYMENT HISTORY
Revenue Agent, Internal Revenue Service, Santa Barbara, CA   1978-86
Accountant, Controller's Office, State of California, Santa Barbara, CA   1974-78

RONALD PAUL GUTHRIE
PO Box 118
Newport Beach, CA 90041
(714) 255-1111

Objective: A Securities Analyst/Management position

PROFESSIONAL EXPERIENCE

MSI SECURITIES, Newport Beach, California   1986-present
Securities Analyst (1990-present)
- Manage over 60 million dollars in tax free debt securities.
- Research the bond market daily to find highest yield available.
- Use Lotus to structure clients' maturity schedule within a 1-5 year range.
- Educate clients concerning MSI investment philosophy.
- Establish relationships with brokerage houses across the nation.

Account Executive (1988-89)
- Responsible for over 300 client accounts.
- Provide client services with quarterly financial reviews, practice management advice, structuring a specific pension plan to meet client's retirement needs.
- Plan annual funding of pension plans, fee review, employee relations, consolidation of debt, and profitability monitors.

Coordinator (1986-87)
- Performed as the conduit between new clients and the entire firm.
- Conducted preliminary analysis of new client's financial material.
- Worked directly with Senior Consultant to create a financial structure to lead client to economic freedom.

EDUCATION

MA Degree, Accounting, 1990
University of Florida, Gainesville, FL

BA, Liberal Arts, 1986
University of Florida, Gainesville, FL

ESTHER S. MICHELLE
1209 Mountain Avenue
Ft. Collins, CO 80524
(303) 223-9584

OBJECTIVE
A Securities Trader position

PROFESSIONAL EXPERIENCE

SECURITIES TRADER
STP Broker Corporation, Denver, CO   1985-present
- Purchase and sell securities for brokerage firm.

- Receive sales order ticket from Registered Representative and inspect form to ensure accuracy of information.

- Contact securities exchange or brokerage firm that is trading requested securities to execute client orders for purchase or sale of securities.

- Complete transaction independently if brokerage firm is market maker in requested securities.

- Record and approve securities transactions.

- Review all securities transactions to ensure that trades conform to regulations of Securities and Exchange Commission, National Association of Securities Dealers, and other government agencies.

- Prepare financial reports to monitor corporate finances.

EDUCATION
MBA, Accounting, 1978
University of Hartford, CT

BA, Accounting, 1974
University of Denver, Denver, CO

LICENSE
Series 7 License: 1974
States of Colorado & Connecticut

PREVIOUS EMPLOYMENT HISTORY
Securities Trader, K & L Broker's Exchange, Hartford, CT   1978-85

MARIANNE SUE TOTTLE
PO Box 89301
Santa Barbara, CA 93190
(805) 569-1020

OBJECTIVE: A Stockbroker position

WORK EXPERIENCE:

DEAN WITTER REYNOLDS, Los Angeles, CA   1988-present
Account Executive
Received Series 7 and Insurance License in 1988. Established over 100 new account relationships. Raised over $1.5M in new equity. Developed Retirement Planning Team concept for branch office, focusing on institutional and individual qualified plan assets. Extensive financial research and analysis based on balance sheets, annual reports, and cash flow figures. Specialize in marketing of mutual funds, equity products, unit trusts and life insurance.

SANWA BANK, Los Angeles, CA   1987-88
Assistant to Vice President of Marketing
Assisted with daily management of over 65 cold callers for Account Executives. Led recruiting, hiring, firing, and training. Managed personnel and office operations. Negotiated contracts for office space, and computer purchases, establishing a new branch office. Promoted to managerial assignment. Supervised spreadsheet analysis and data entry of all marketing research.

JOHNSON, TAMBARELLO, STEIN, Beverly Hills, CA   1985-87
Broker's Assistant
Assisted with prospecting and follow up on clients. Researched Financial and Marketing analysis. Experience with various Macintosh and IBM programs.

EDUCATION:

BA Degree, Accounting
University of Southern California
Emphasis: International Economics
Graduation: 1987

HONORS:

University Scholarship, University of Southern California
USC, Academic and Financial National Elks Scholarship
Elected Treasurer, International Business Association

CHARLIE O. THOM
1243 E. Elizabeth Street
Ft. Collins, CO 80524
(303) 224-5540

OBJECTIVE
A Tax Accountant Manager position

PROFESSIONAL EXPERIENCE

SENIOR TAX ACCOUNTANT   1985-present
J & L Accounting Services

- Prepare federal, state, and local tax returns for businesses throughout Larimer County.

- Examine accounts and records and compute taxes owed according to prescribed rates, laws, and regulations, using a highly sophisticated computerized accounting system.

- Advise management regarding effects of business activities on taxes, and on strategies for minimizing tax liability.

- Ensure that each business complies with periodic tax payment, information reporting, and other taxing authority requirements.

- Represent principal before taxing bodies.

- Specialize in small business and partnership income tax preparation.

EDUCATION

BBA, Accounting, 1978
University of Texas at Austin

PREVIOUS EMPLOYMENT HISTORY

Staff Tax Accountant, Business Accounting Service, Ft. Collins, CO   1981-85
Staff Tax Accountant, Jordan Income Tax Service, Ft. Collins, CO   1978-81

RACHEL P. GROVES, C.P.A.
3209 Galway Street
Ft. Collins, CO 80521
(303) 221-9948

OBJECTIVE
Tax Auditor

PROFESSIONAL EXPERIENCE

Dickson & Associates, Ft. Collins, CO   1986-present
TAX AUDITOR
- Audit financial records to determine tax liability for large and small businesses throughout Larimer County.

- Review material assets, income, surpluses, liabilities, and expenditures from taxpayer to verify net worth or reported financial status and identify potential tax issues.

- Analyze issues to determine nature, scope, and direction of investigation required.

- Develop and evaluate evidence of taxpayer finances to determine tax liability, using knowledge of interest and discount, annuities, valuation of stocks and bonds, sinking funds, and amortization valuation of depletable assets.

- Prepare written explanation of findings to notify taxpayer of tax liability.

- Advise taxpayer of appeal rights.

EDUCATION
MBA, Accounting, 1978
University of Alabama at Birmingham

BA, Accounting, 1974
University of Denver, Denver, CO

PREVIOUS EMPLOYMENT HISTORY
Certified Public Accountant, Thomas & Associates, Birmingham, AL   1978-83
Certified Public Accountant, Hogan, Goodwin & Company, Denver, CO   1974-78

JESSE O. RAPHAEL
432 E. Elizabeth Street
Ft. Collins, CO 80524
(303) 224-5432

OBJECTIVE
A Tax Manager position

PROFESSIONAL EXPERIENCE
TAX MANAGER   1985-present
Jules Corporation, Denver, CO
- Work closely with the Controller to direct the tax accounting staff responsible for determining the corporate liability to taxing authorities.

- Delegate income tax, licenses, sales tax, property tax and payroll tax functions to tax accounting staff.

- Analyze the effects of tax accounting alternatives and study laws and regulations to insure correct application of new tax measures.

PROFESSIONAL AFFILIATIONS
Member, American Accounting Association
Member, National Association of Tax Practitioners

EDUCATION
MBA, Accounting, 1978
California State University, Los Angeles

BA, Accounting, 1974
University of Denver, Denver, CO

PREVIOUS EMPLOYMENT HISTORY
Tax Consultant, Charles & Taylor Associates, Los Angeles, CA   1978-85
Tax Associate, The Medical Foundation, Denver, CO   1974-78

ROGER PAUL HOUSTON, C.P.A.
1043 Maple Court
Ft. Collins, CO 80524
(303) 224-5432

OBJECTIVE
Tax Manager

PROFESSIONAL EXPERIENCE

TAX MANAGER   1988-present
Coopers & Lybrand, Denver, CO
- Direct and review Associate and Senior tax staff.

- Approve corporate tax returns prepared by audit staff.

- Consult with audit staff when questions arise.

- Perform tax planning and preparation for individuals, estates, trusts, and small businesses.

- Research any unusual tax matters.

PROFESSIONAL AFFILIATIONS
Member, American Accounting Association
Member, American Institute of Certified Public Accountants

EDUCATION
MBA, Accounting, 1988
California State University, Los Angeles

BA, Accounting, 1982
University of Denver, Denver, CO
C.P.A. Exam: Passed 1980

PREVIOUS EMPLOYMENT HISTORY
Senior Tax Associate, Coopers & Lybrand, Los Angeles, CA   1985-88
Tax Associate, Thomas & Associates, Denver, CO   1982-85

HARVEY J. SOUIX, C.P.A.
1239 Horsetooth Road
Ft. Collins, CO 80525
(303) 225-5432

OBJECTIVE
Tax Manager

PROFESSIONAL EXPERIENCE

SENIOR TAX ASSOCIATE   1988-present
Price Waterhouse, Denver, CO
• Prepare and review income tax returns for individuals and corporations.

• Counsel clients on a variety of tax issues.

• Research tax questions, offer suggestions for tax planning and study tax laws
  for potential tax savings for corporate and individual clients.

• Use the microcomputer on tax research and compliance projects.

• Train and supervise new tax associate staff members.

PROFESSIONAL AFFILIATIONS
Member, American Accounting Association
Member, American Institute of Certified Public Accountants

EDUCATION
MBA, Accounting, 1988
California State University, Los Angeles

BA, Accounting, 1984
University of Denver, Denver, CO
C.P.A. Exam: Passed 1984

PREVIOUS EMPLOYMENT HISTORY
Tax Associate, Price Waterhouse, Los Angeles, CA   1984-88
Accounting Intern, Price Waterhouse, Denver, CO   1982-84

SOMOYA L. HASSAN
1235 Eastman Street
Ft. Collins, CO 80526
(303) 226-3330

OBJECTIVE
A Securities Trader position

PROFESSIONAL EXPERIENCE

FLOOR TRADER   1986-present
AFP Stock Exchange, Denver, CO
- Buy and sell fixed income securities on floor based on market quotation and competition in market.

- Analyze market conditions and trends to determine best time to execute securities transaction orders.

- Inform registered representative of market fluctuations and securities transactions affecting accounts.

- Specialize in trading corporates, governments, municipals, foreigns, and mortgages.

EDUCATION
MBA, Accounting, 1978
University of Hartford, CT

BA, Accounting, 1974
University of Denver, Denver, CO

LICENSE
Series 7 License: 1974
States of Colorado & Connecticut

PREVIOUS EMPLOYMENT HISTORY

Trader, Hartford Stock Exchange, Hartford, CT   1978-86
Financial Planner, Denver Bank & Trust, Denver, CO   1974-78

RANDOLPH P. NICHOLS
2165 Dunbar Street
Ft. Collins, CO 80525
(303) 223-9487

OBJECTIVE
The Treasurer for a Nonprofit Organization

PROFESSIONAL EXPERIENCE

TREASURER   1982-present
Nonprofit Organization of Ft. Collins, Ft. Collins, CO

* Direct financial planning, procurement, and investment of funds.

* Delegate authority for receipt, disbursement, banking, protection and custody of funds, securities, and financial instruments.

* Analyze financial records to forecast future financial position and budget requirements.

* Evaluate need for procurement of funds and investment of surplus.

* Advise management on investments and loans for short- and long-range financial plans.

* Prepare financial reports for management.

* Develop policies and procedures for account collections and extension of credit to customers.

* Sign notes of indebtedness as approved by management.

EDUCATION
MBA, Accounting, 1978
University of Hartford, CT

BA, Accounting, 1970
University of Denver, Denver, CO

PREVIOUS EMPLOYMENT HISTORY

Assistant Treasurer, United Way of Hartford, CT	1976-82
Treasury Operations Analyst, Bank of Colorado, Denver, CO	1973-76
Staff Cash Manager, Bank of Denver, Denver, CO	1970-73

MALLORY MARIE GALVISTON
59 Martinella Drive
Montecito, CA 93108
(805) 966-0845

Objective: Trust Administrator

PROFESSIONAL EXPERIENCE

Trust Administration & Marketing
- Managed 180 accounts with total market value of $150M; revenues of $1.4M: Living...Testamentary...Conservatorship...Unitrusts...Agency...Custody.
- Launched intensive Cohen-Brown marketing techniques including financial profiling of existing client base, branch contact and organizing seminars.
- Organized highly successful in-house marketing campaigns that created excitement, promoted sales and generated new business for the bank.
- Conducted a week-long training seminar on new Trust Aid procedures for our updated in-house computer system.
- Prepared discretionary requests and monitored investments, distributions, terminations and sale of personal property.
- Served as portfolio manager for accounts fully vested in Common Trust Funds.
- Gained valuable business contacts through interbank communication and correspondence with attorneys, brokers, and accountants in the trust industry.

Probate Paralegal
- Responsible for file management and factual investigation.
- Discovered, collected and distributed assets.
- Prepared and processed pleadings, federal/state estate, gift and inheritance tax and income tax returns, probate accountings and narrative descriptions.
- Interfaced with secretarial, word processing, accounting and other support departments.

EDUCATION
Certified Financial Planner, 1990
College of Financial Planning, Denver, CO

Paralegal, Certified: 1982
The Institute of Paralegal Training
Philadelphia, PA

BA, Business Economics, 1980
University of Arizona, Tucson, AZ

EMPLOYMENT HISTORY
Trust Administrator, Wells Fargo Bank, Santa Barbara, CA	1987-present
Trust Administrator, Union Bank, Los Angeles, CA	1985-87
Probate Paralegal, Sheppard, Mullin, Hampton, Lyne, CA	1983-85
Probate Paralegal, Rooks, Pitts, & Poust, Chicago, IL	1982-83

WALTER B. STEIN
3214 Mountain Avenue
Ft. Collins, CO 80524
(303) 224-9547

OBJECTIVE
Underwriter

PROFESSIONAL EXPERIENCE
UNDERWRITER
<u>Capital Insurance Corporation</u>, Ft. Collins, CO   1985-present
* Specialize in multiline insurance, pensions and workers' compensation.

* Review insurance applications to evaluate, classify, and rate individuals and groups for insurance.

* Examine application form, inspection report, insurance maps, and medical reports to determine degree of risk.

* Review company records to determine amount of insurance in force on single risk or group of closely related risks, and evaluate possibility of losses.

* Write to field representative, medical personnel, and other insurance companies to obtain further information, quote rates, or explain company policies.

* Decline excessive risks. Authorize reinsurance of policy when risk is high.

* Decrease value of policy when risk is substandard to limit company obligation, and specify applicable endorsements.

PROFESSIONAL AFFILIATIONS
Member, <u>American Underwriters' Association</u>

EDUCATION
MBA, Accounting, 1978
<u>California State University, Los Angeles</u>

BA, Accounting, 1974
<u>University of Denver</u>, Denver, CO

PREVIOUS EMPLOYMENT HISTORY
Internal Auditor, <u>The California Bar Association</u>, Los Angeles, CA   1976-85
Internal Auditor, <u>Law Offices of Geoffrey & Stone</u>, Denver, CO   1974-76

Index to Resume Samples by Job Title

Subject Index

If you're not looking here, you're hardly looking.

There are lots of publications you can turn to when you're looking for a job. But in today's tough job market, you need the National Business Employment Weekly. It not only lists hundreds of high-paying jobs available now at major corporations all across the country, it also gives you valuable strategies and advice to help you land one of those jobs. NBEW is a Wall Street Journal publication. It's the leading national job-search and career guidance publication and has been for over ten years. Pick it up at your newsstand today. Or get the next 12 issues delivered first class for just $52 by calling toll-free...

800-367-9600

National Business Employment Weekly
If you're not looking here, you're hardly looking.